Faces of Poverty,
Faces of Christ

Faces of Poverty, Faces of Christ

John F. Kavanaugh

Photographs by Mev Puleo

ORBIS BOOKS

Maryknoll, New York 10545

Some of the chapters, in modified form, have appeared in the *Saint Louis Review*. The author is especially thankful for the encouragement and uncommon, skilled generosity of Robert Ellsberg, Editor-in-Chief of Orbis Books.

The Catholic Foreign Mission Society of America (Maryknoll) recruits and trains people for overseas missionary service. Through Orbis Books, Maryknoll aims to foster the international dialogue that is essential to mission. The books published, however, reflect the opinions of their authors and are not meant to represent the official position of the society.

Library of Congress Cataloging-in-Publication Data

Kavanaugh, John F.
    Faces of poverty, faces of Christ / John F. Kavanaugh;
photographs by Mev Puleo.
      p. cm.
    ISBN 0-88344-725-8
    1. Poverty — Religious aspects — Christianity — Meditations.
2. Kavanaugh, John F. I. Title.
BV4647.P6K38 1991
261.8′325 — dc20
                                    90-21514
                                      CIP

To the faces of the photographs
and the heroes of the stories,
especially the "toe woman"
and her friend, Julia

Contents

Contents

Foreword

by Jean Vanier

My brother,
My sister,
I ask you to read these pages
carefully,
slowly,
prayerfully.
Take time
to look at the faces
and listen to the words.
Let these faces and words
sink into your heart and mind and flesh
and awaken the murmurings of the Spirit.

In this book, John Kavanaugh reveals a secret,
the secret of the Gospels:
God is hidden in those realities
we most often shun,
and run from:
people who are broken and in pain;
our own brokenness, our own pain.
Yes, God is truly present
in the wondrous beauty of the universe,
in the skies and sun and stars,
in beautiful liturgies
and in all our noble activities.

And yet, God is truly present
in a very special way,
in all that is apparently ugly,
all that stinks
and is broken.

These pages are calling you to enter into this secret.
Do not flee from people who are broken and in pain!
Walk toward them!
Walk with them!
Perhaps you will approach them as a healer.
You will be surprised, then, to discover
that as you walk with them
you yourself are being transformed and healed.
John shows that through being with broken people,
our own brokenness is uncovered.
This is the road to truth and to wholeness.
Thus we live the Cross as the road to resurrection.

Who can believe such folly?
It is the folly of the message of Jesus.
A message of hope,
a message of truth,
a message that can bring peace
if we take the risk of becoming a follower of Jesus.
Do we really believe that
"God chose what is foolish in the world
to shame the wise;
God chose what is weak in the world
to shame the strong;
God chose what is low and even despised in the world—
even things that are not." (I Cor. 1:27–29)
These last twenty-six years,
living in community with men and women
who have a mental handicap
have show me the truth of these words
and of this book.

INTRODUCTION

The Five Faces of Poverty

In the fall of 1983, I found myself, with two hundred other Jesuits, in Saint Peter's Basilica, listening to the Beatitudes.

The fact that it was the "tough" version of the Beatitudes—"Blessed are the poor ... but woe to you who are rich"—made the irony almost embarrassing.

Here we were, one of the wealthiest communities of men in the wealthiest of religions in the world, convened at great cost, laden with doctorates and simultaneous translators, surrounded by opulence of art and artifice, listening to the Beatitudes.

Then Fr. Peter Hans Kolvenbach, the Superior General of the Society of Jesus, gave a stirring homily, which in some ways met the irony head on. But it was not without the price of surfacing once again the daunting paradoxes and ambiguities that are one with the reality of poverty.

His words were literally confounding:

Only when we come to live out our consecration to the Kingdom in a communion that is for the poor, with the poor, and against all forms of human poverty, material and spiritual, only then, will the poor see that the gates of the Kingdom are open to them.

But what can these words mean?

How can you be "with and for the poor" and at the same time "against all forms of poverty"? Why is it advisable to embrace "material poverty" if one hopes to combat it? How are we to be against all forms of "spiritual" poverty, when poverty of spirit is the prerequisite for receiving the Kingdom of God?

This quandary embodies not only much of the confusion about poverty, simplicity, the preferential option for the poor, and spiritual poverty in the world today; it also represents a central struggle with the reality of poverty as it is encountered in the gospels.

A wealthy man says, "Come off it, Father. Wealth is good. Nobody wants to be poor, especially churches. Why make it 'blessed'?"

A student complains, "If Jesus said 'blessed are the poor,' and 'the poor you will always have with you,' then why are you trying to make them well-off?"

A teacher in an affluent secondary school says, "My poor are right here."

A community superior intones, "You can find the poor in our very community; why not attend to them?"

Two married professionals worry, "Does the preferential option for the poor mean that you are leaving us out?"

All the confusion could well be a massive evasion, especially by church-people, businesspersons, and citizens in a culture almost suffocating in wealth. We can easily use the ambiguities concerning poverty to excuse ourselves from entering its reality.

But it may not all be due to hardness of heart. The face of poverty is found in so many roles, reflected in so many mirrors, the effect can be dizzying.

Poverty is an issue of social justice. Poverty is also a traditional religious vow. It has something to do with both greed and the condition of oppression. It has something to do with both simplicity and consumerist myths. At times it seems to be a high spiritual gift. But it also seems appropriate to use it as the word to describe spiritual death.

We offer this book as an attempt to face poverty in its various forms, to meet poverty in its multiple faces.

Thus, our many words, our many images, range over five different realms of poverty.

There is a negative material poverty which dehumanizes us.

There is a positive material poverty, that of simplicity, which humanizes us.

There is a negative spiritual poverty of sin which degrades us.

And there is a positive spiritual poverty which ennobles us.

In all, there is a fifth face that shines in ten thousand places. It is the face of the Poor Christ of the Poor God who hears the Cry of the Poor.

We will experience the liberating reality of poverty and its centrality to the life of Christian faith only if we recognize this "fifth" face, mirrored in the other four.

We cannot shun one of his faces and still encounter the whole Christ.

We cannot ignore or suppress his presence in any of poverty's faces and then hope to find him.

If we open our eyes and hearts to this truth, it will not constrain or defeat us; it will set us free.

And we might finally understand why the poor—even we ourselves—are blessed.

I

DEHUMANIZING
MATERIAL POVERTY

Then the king will say to those on his right hand,
"Come, you whom my father has blessed,
take for your heritage the kingdom prepared for you
since the foundation of the world.
For I was hungry and you gave me food;
naked and you clothed me
sick and you visited me
in prison and you came to see me."

Then the virtuous will say to him in reply,
"Lord, when did we see you hungry and feed you;
or thirsty and give you drink?
When did we see you a stranger and make you welcome;
naked and clothe you;
sick or in prison and go to see you?"

And the king will answer,
"I tell you solemnly,
insofar as you did this to one of the least of
these brothers and sisters of mine,
you did it to me."

— Matthew 25:34–40

Degradation

There is a poverty which is not blessed.

It is a curse.

It is a privation, a hole that exists only as a parasite of wholeness.

This is a form of "material" poverty which can be seen as the result of both physical and moral evil.

It is the price of fallible time and the painful organic growth exacted by the earthquakes and tidal waves in the march of the earth.

It is the price of fallible humanity, paid in the coinage of sin, of chosen wars, concocted reichs, and contrived tyrannies.

It can crush the spirit.

Its fruit is death. The extinction of life. The last objectification of persons. Entropy.

Christ came not to bless this poverty, but to change it.

He did not bless death. He accepted it only to transform it.

He felt this godforsakeness: not to recommend it, but to fight through it and have it overcome.

He came that war might end, that earthquakes might be tamed and healed.

He came to challenge all that would degrade and dehumanize human beings, to eliminate the grinding and blinding poverties that make us alien even from ourselves, that imprison and suffocate, that render us mute objects, that oppress and mutilate the spirit.

This was his mission: to bring good news to such poor, because this kind of poverty must be transformed.

He would tell the disciples of John to report the findings: the blind see,

3

the halt walk, and the poor have the Good News preached to them.

Finally, so much would he want this dehumanizing poverty changed, he revealed that our response to such degradation would be the very condition of our entry into his reign:

> whether we had fed the starving
> whether we had clothed the naked
> whether we had housed the alien and homeless
> whether we had reached out to the criminal
> whether we had offered our cup of grace to the thirsts of humankind.

So much did he want the sufferings of these poor attended to that he took upon himself their skin and bones.

And told us we would be attending to him.

Mother Teresa

I first met Mother Teresa at six in the morning. I was saying Mass in the Calcutta motherhouse and she was coming to Communion.

"Wait till they hear about this back home. I gave Communion to Mother Teresa."

But then she gazed at the host to receive it; and I forgot about back home.

Her intensity and presence literally made me feel that I was holding the Body of Christ.

I had always thought I believed it. But now, believing it was another matter.

I felt this strange invasion of faith only once before: giving Communion to Jean Vanier. For some reason, the radical implications of our eucharistic faith are made concrete, given flesh, by such people. When Vanier or Mother Teresa received Communion, you knew they were really receiving something. And when they received you, you felt the same.

There would be more.

At the House of the Dying, Kalighat, we had a shriveled old Hindu who had been on the cot nearest the door for three weeks.

He was supposed to have been the next to die, but he lingered. Collapsed into a fetal hug, he made no response, never spoke, never ate a thing.

It was this man that Mother Teresa first visited upon a return to Calcutta. She would always go first to the House of the Dying and then stop at the cot nearest the door. Here she thought she would see the one nearest to heaven.

She knelt down.

She took his face into her hands.

Her movements could only be compared to those when receiving Communion.

He opened his eyes.

He smiled at her.

She fed him.

There are two sacraments of transubstantiation, each incomprehensible to empiricism, each an assault upon received pragmatic wisdom, each devastating to utilitarian sensibilities.

"This is my Body." And we humans, so hungry for existence, are fed with the life of God.

"This is my Body." And we humans, so blessed with existence, are empowered to feed God—now, no longer under the appearance of bread and wine, but of flesh and blood.

Terror

"Why does your country continue to support my government which is committing atrocities against my people?"

The man who asked me that question a few years ago in Rome is now dead — himself a victim of atrocity — at the hands of a government supported by our own and touted as a model of democracy.

Ignacio Ellacuría, S.J., the president of the University of Central America in San Salvador, along with his vice-president, four other Jesuit professors, a community cook and her teenage daughter, was tortured, riddled with bullets and mutilated early the morning of November 16, 1989.

There were witnesses, no doubt in hiding as were so many other Salvadorans on that day, their city being bombed by their own military, their homes being strafed by the ominously terrifying helicopters and rockets.

Despite our State Department's evasions, despite the claims that "no one takes responsibility," the story will be told. These eight people, like so many of the other seventy thousand Salvadorans who have been killed in the last decade, were assassinated by forces which are directly supported by the United States of America.

"Why does your country continue to support my government which is committing atrocities against my people?"

And so, Ignacio Ellacuría's words stay with me.

He was 59. He entered the Jesuits in Spain when he was 17 and spent most of the last thirty years as a missionary in El Salvador. He was a passionate man. Often during those meetings in Rome he would speak long and tirelessly of the oppressed and of the gospel requirement to stand in solidarity with the poor.

He was also a man of intelligence, adept in seven languages, the author of seven books bearing titles such as *Freedom Made Flesh*, *Faith and Justice*, and *The Crucified People*.

In Rome I saw a list with his and others' names on it. It was a "death list" from Central America. He had been warned countless times not to speak out against the ruling government, not to be a trouble-maker, but he would not be silenced or intimidated.

If anything, he and his brothers felt *too* protected—concerned that they did not really share the peril of the poor and the "disappeared." Being professors at a university, surely their government would not try to put an end to them, if only for the appearance of normalcy and civilization. The poor might be wiped out without notice, but not priests and professors.

They were wrong. Like 70,000 nameless of the last decade killed in El Salvador, they are now statistics. And my own country is still not ashamed.

One wonders what our State Department would proclaim if six priests were killed in Poland. One wonders what threats would be made if they were killed by Sandinistas.

But here was *our* "model democracy" at work. And so our public pronouncements lamely suggest that we do not know the perpetrators of the crime.

Even though for three days prior to the murders the Salvadoran state and military radio had been making threats that the Jesuits were marked for murder.

Even though the killers miraculously passed through military barricades.

Even though the victims were on a right-wing "death list" for seven years.

Perhaps the Government and the Army felt secure.

This was the week, after all, when the United States Congress budgeted $85 million in military aid to Salvador and $12 million for police training—as part of a yearly $400 million package.

This was the day that the *New York Times* could quote the Bush Administration as having "full confidence" in President Alfredo Christiani. But Christiani was the handpicked choice of the Arena Party and its mastermind, Roberto D'Aubuisson, the man described by a former U.S. ambassador as a "pathological killer."

D'Aubuisson's forces have been linked, not only to the deaths of Archbishop Oscar Romero and four North American religious women, but also to the deaths of so many others who have gone unnoticed.

Ignacio Ellacuría may well be happy now that a moment's attention is given to the endless suffering of the Salvadoran people and that finally he and his brothers are no longer more secure and protected than the poor.

Like others, he had been called a subversive—which he was not. After all, President Christiani himself acknowledged this.

But even if such lies were true, the military and police could at least have arrested him and brought him to trial.

They didn't have to slaughter a woman witness and her child.

They didn't have to round up six men in the early morning hours and fill them with bullets.

They didn't have to shoot out their brains.

That last act, as horribly symbolic as it was, will not extinguish the spirit of Ignacio Ellacuría and his seven companions in death. His fine and earnest mind remains to question us all:

"Why does your country continue to support my government which is committing atrocities against my people?"

Johanna

The mystery of God's marriage with humanity invites an utter reliance upon such a God who would desire our existence so much as to become one with our flesh.

The mysticism of the Word made human flesh, moreover, is at the same time a spirituality of utter resistance to the forces of human degradation — as ancient as sin, as modern as missiles.

We rely, not on Caesar and Mars, but on God.

Not in armies are we saved, not by the uncontrollable appetite to consume more pleasures and collect more securities, not by the chains of the capitalist or communist illusions.

We are saved in the Blood of Jesus Christ. Our bodies have become his very own.

This is our hope. This is our trust. This is our security.

Johanna, a young nurse and former student, felt that saving reality.

She was awakened one dark morning in her inner-city apartment by someone shaking her in her bed.

Standing over her was a man brandishing a knife.

She would later tell me that all she could think of saying was, "I place myself entirely in the hands of Jesus Christ."

After twenty minutes of stark silence, the man mute in staring at her, she spoke the words again: "I place myself in the hands of Jesus Christ."

His voice finally broke the still terror:

"If I leave quietly, will you let me go?"

If we unconditionally give ourselves to the mystery of Christ's Blood poured out, we experience the reality of being saved and the absoluteness of radical trust.

But our yielding to the truth of our own preciousness in the eyes of God unleashes a most radical freedom in our lives.

Thus, the acceptance of the truth of our being loved is the launching of our mission.

The Christmas after the intruder-incident, Johanna wrote to me of her work as a nurse among the poor of the South:

> The fulfillment of the human person grounded in the Gospel of Christ is not borne out in mere plans and future events, but in the love that can be shown to the marvel of God's creation—the human person—in daily events. My profession, nursing, is such a gift in this respect—each day to be given the privilege of touching, comforting, teaching the person of Christ in each patient! Even the malformed or the bedridden or the emotionally crippled or those who suffer greatly—they all bear the countenance of our glorious God. I have been given the gift of seeing the resurrected Christ juxtaposed with him suffering in the same person.
>
> God is so good.

If we have wholly accepted the truth of our salvation, of our being infinitely valued in the eyes of God, we then become empowered to enter into the fullest mystery of Holy Communion.

Jesus has said, "This is my Body, this is my Blood," not only over the bread and the wine, but over the body and blood of men and women. When we fully enter into his saving mystery, we begin to see each other as God sees us.

We look at even the least of our brothers and sisters and see the Body and Blood of Christ.

We see each other as God sees us. But this is not that we may save each other.

It is that we may serve each other.

Bill Wilson

It was three weeks after the fact that I found out Bill Wilson had died. White. Male. About 40 years old.

The people in the hotel didn't know who he was, so it took the police 20 days to finally contact his mother in another state.

There were seven of us at the memorial Mass. Somebody commented that Bill had experienced enough hell on earth, so he wouldn't be suffering much now. It was said with relief.

Bill had been feeling part of that "hell" a little over a year ago when, screaming over the phone at 2 A.M., he begged me to come to his rooming house to take on the devil who had invaded his room.

What do you do with such a person? He had had one good (rare) year out of jails and institutions, become a Catholic, even felt one day that God did indeed love him as he was contemplating the crucifix in the College Church. But now he was coming apart again — still not drinking, but wanting to write his life story from those musty cassette tapes or wanting to open a storefront psychologist's office at cut rates.

So on the phone he was blowing his top. Here he's a Catholic being taunted by the devil and he can't even get a priest to help him out!

I was as fearful as he was angry. I tried to help him but only at the comfortable distance that a phone could afford.

The next day he seemed calmer, but also more remote. I knew it would be only a matter of time before he would be back in the City lockup or State Psychiatric.

The next months were terrible. He spent them (when he was not being treated for injuries at City Hospital) at City Jail. Like so many times before — due to the brutality of the system and his own violence against himself — he came unglued. I was always relieved when the jail guards would not let me see Bill. I could go home with the satisfaction of having tried without having to see his burnt and bruised body, without having to try to make sense of his ravings, without having to explain why I wasn't allowed to bring him a package of Kools or a portable radio.

He bottomed out during those weeks in "solitary hole." The guards would let me peek in through a three-inch slot. I had never seen a man look so much like a wild animal, so physically desperate, so jumpy with fear and hate.

He wanted Confession, Communion, just to talk, to write letters, to get lawyers, to escape, to get the ACLU, to get money, to get even, to kill the guards.

I couldn't wait to leave.

He couldn't bear to see me go.

So it was.

One of those visiting days, as I was getting into the car, a woman shyly asked me if I was a friend of Wilson. Her brother (a con who was being transferred to Fulton) said that Bill was regularly beaten every night by the guards.

Old Bill was telling the truth. It was at this time that one of the inmates at City Jail died from "falling from his bunk during the night." And it was soon after this that the astute Attorney General of the United States made the statement that only the rich went to jail.

After six months or so, Bill finally got his trial. He was cleaned up and treated nicely for the last few weeks so that the blackened eyes faded and the welts left his face. And soon he was out again. After a night at Harbor Lights, he was back into a rooming house, back into the heavy drinking, the purported cause of death: alcohol poisoning.

Bill, dear Bill.

At your Resurrection Mass some of your friends tried to recall a few of those good times you may have had, a few of those laughs, a few of the clear and possibly happy months.

Sure, there were a few times like that.

But I recall—even though bittersweet—what you did for me.

Having few pretenses of your own left, you crashed through so many of the protections endemic to my character and fostered by the clerical state, by privilege, by theorizing. You revealed my blindness and helped me see more than rooming houses and dives. You helped me be a little less frozen when I think of jails—including the ones I inhabit. You cut away some of the downtroddenness of fear and spurious security.

I did not find the learning easy. I resisted the news. But you stuck with it.

And remember, somewhere it is written that this itself was the mission of Jesus, what you did for me. Some people think he comes in fine-fashioned words, homilies, and smiles.

I think he comes at least as frequently in speechless prison cells, from panhandlers, and shrill phone calls at 2 A.M.

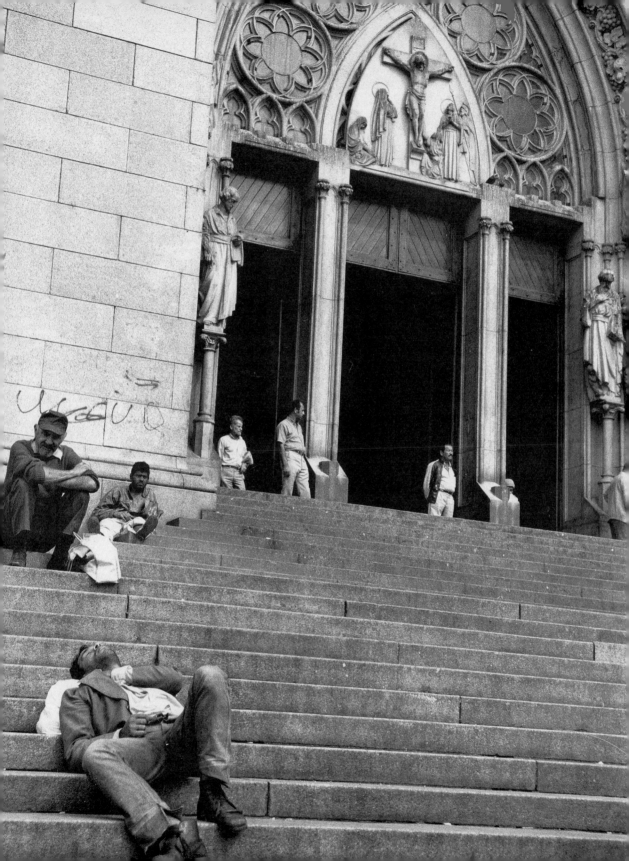

Precious Blood

The central reality of the Incarnation: God in Flesh.

Precious Blood.

Preciousness and blood.

But not today. Not in the modern world.

If anything, today, human blood is cheap.

Despite all the rhetoric to the contrary, the reality is that the blood of persons is valueless.

We waste it: institutionally, clinically and deliberately, on our death rows.

We spill it in the delivery rooms of hospitals—from St. Louis to Bombay, from Warsaw to Peking.

We wipe out a million and a half of the unborn in one year alone in the United States.

We cannot manage a sigh of sorrow for 290 souls shot out of the sky by our eager mistakes.

We contemplate wars for the sake of over-abundant oil.

The starving of millions scarcely merits a shrug.

And nations glut themselves with munitions readied for the murder of millions more.

No, blood is not precious in the modern world.

If anything, now more than ever, it serves as a frightening symbol of evil. Contamination by needles, remnant blots from murder in the streets, the withering-away of persons.

The unclean shame of blood has new meaning. It is not just the sign of our terrible contingency.

It is the hallmark of fear.

And human flesh is not only frail. It is forgotten. Lost in the rubble of Lebanon, passed over by the helicopters of Salvador, left behind by the clever Stealth bomber.

Flesh is buried in the graves of Kampuchea.

Flesh is crushed by the tanks of Tiananmen Square.

And yet our sacramental sensibility resists such degrading of flesh and blood.

Our faith is so physical, our Transcendent so Incarnate.

Our deepest communal impulse is to celebrate conceptions and births, covenants and martyrdoms, a Sacred Heart, the Corpus Christi, the holy wounds, the mystical body.

At the instant of our most holy of communions, around the world, the words are heard, "Body of Christ."

Among our most precious consecrations, from our earliest beginnings, over millions of utterances, through hundreds of languages:

"This is the cup of my Blood, the blood of the new and everlasting covenant, shed for you and for all, that sins may be forgiven."

The Incarnation, the Birth, the Death and Resurrection of Jesus Christ, true God and true human, has made all human blood precious.

The eternal Creator looks at the least human person and now not only numbers the hairs of our head—but sanctifies our every drop of blood.

God looks at the least and sees the eternal Child of God, Jesus—sees the Word made flesh and blood. We are saved in him.

In Jesus, God says over the least human being, God gives the word, "This is my Body and Blood." Jesus is the Holy Communion, the Transubstantiation of humanity.

Thus to exact blood of the criminal, to destroy it in the unborn, to plan its spillage in the ranks of our enemies, to ignore its drying up in the faces of the impoverished, to intend its loss in our manufacturing and marketing of arms, to fail to mourn its pouring out of those we deem expendable—all this is sacrilege.

Our mission of justice and service is not a mission of liberalism or the pet project of social activists. It is a mission to the Precious Blood and Body. It is a devotion to the Blood of Christ in the very persons whom Christ intends to save by his identification with them.

To be devoted to the project of ending human degradation is not a pastime of religious faith. It is a commitment to stop the sacrilege.

For it is the Body and Blood of Christ, of God made human flesh, which is degraded in dehumanizing poverty.

> To stop the sacrilege is
> to feed their great hunger, which is his;
> to shelter them, for it is his homelessness;
> to visit them in prison, for he abides there;
> to challenge all institutions which degrade persons, for it is
> his Body and Blood which has made them precious.

After the Passion, Death and Resurrection of Jesus, our blood, no matter what the blind violence of sinful men and women might indicate, was never again to be seen as something cheap.

It was so precious that God would die for it.

And our blood would never again be our shame or fear.

Rather, it would become the sign of God's covenantal love for us and the unbreakable promise of eternal life.

This is the conviction behind the Christian's challenge to a world so violent that one might think humans have nothing precious about them at all.

The eternal word of God, now flesh, dwells among us.

"This is my Body," he said.

"This is my Blood."

"Do this in memory of me."

The Street

I saw her first out of the corner of my eye.
I tried to move as fast as I could.
My tickets to Delhi were fresh bought and I had to rest before leaving.

The trick is not to look them in the eye.
To keep moving.
Not to catch their glance.
In fact, I'm told, most of them are fakes. They even make themselves
look miserable for the sake of a rupee.

I had gotten past the man with no arms or legs. He was a stump that was
twisting his hips to roll along in the gutter, shoving his empty pan with his
head. He was turned downward when I squeezed by, so he didn't see me.

But she did.
And her eyes riveted me.
"Ma"
(does it mean bread or money?).
I usually brought bread or bananas along to give away. But I never gave
money. Rackets, you know. It just encourages them.
"Ma" —
And she looked upon me.
Was she sixty? Both hands out for "Ma."
And before her, on the sidewalk, two baby infants, the size of my hand.
I tore my eyes away.
I really had no time. And at dusk, there would be hundreds more around
me if I stopped to see.

On my way home I thought of the parable of the Good Samaritan.
And how I had lost on all three counts.
I was a priest.
I was a scribe.
I was a teacher.

The Dream

I was back safe.

The Jesuit residence offered friendship and food.

Finally sleep, before the early morning journey to Delhi.

And so I found myself, once again in Howrah Station. It seemed like Babylon. A sea of blankets and smoke.

Thousands move in from the cold streets at night. Their dung fires are a choking obstacle course. Their blankets hide every piece of ground I try to claim for footing.

And then the arms, only arms, reach out to me from under their covers. And "ma" they say.

Will you help?

Will you stay?

Will you abide?

Will you touch?

I explain, it seems, to hundreds: I'm sorry. I'm in such a hurry. And I may miss my train to Delhi. Maybe the next time I'm passing through. But I have to keep moving.

Then the trestle.

I reach it almost gasping, groping to board, to scramble out of the sea of humanity.

Her eyes come into me first.

She emerges like a cartoon board or one of those plastic inflated dolls that flies back up off the floor in reply to all efforts to push it aside.

And she is standing in my way.

She is blocking the entrance to the train car.

Then, the word. Not "ma" but

"Now."

"But I can't help now."

"Now.
If you don't do it now, you never will
Now is the time
Now
Now is the time to live and to love and to labor
Now."

And in defense and argument I awake to know that even if the woman who was poor might be left behind by me, she herself would never abandon this hurried man who was so dangerously close to forgetting the Presence of the Now.

"A Grain of Corn"

I had gone a-begging from door to door in the village path, when thy golden chariot appeared in the distance like a gorgeous dream and I wondered who was this King of all kings!

My hopes rose high and methought my evil days were at an end, and I stood waiting for alms to be given unasked and for wealth scattered on all sides in the dust.

The chariot stopped where I stood. Thy glance fell on me and thou camest down with a smile. I felt the luck of my life had come at last. Then of a sudden thou didst hold out thy right hand and say, "What hast thou to give to me?"

Ah, what a kingly jest was it to open thy palm to a beggar to beg! I was confused and stood undecided, and then from my wallet I slowly took out the least little grain of corn and gave it to thee.

But how great my surprise when at the day's end I emptied my bag on the floor to find a least little grain of gold among the poor heap!

I bitterly wept and wished that I had had the heart to give thee my all.

$-$ R. Tagore
Gitanjali

II

HUMANIZING
MATERIAL POVERTY

These remained faithful to the teaching of the apostles,
to the community,
to the breaking of the bread
and to the prayers.

The many miracles and signs worked through the apostles
made a deep impression on everyone.
The faithful all lived together and owned everything in common.
They sold their goods and possessions
and shared out the proceeds among themselves
according to what each one needed.

They went as a body to the temple every day
but met in their houses for the breaking of the bread.
They shared their food gladly and generously.
They praised God and were looked up to by everyone.

Day by day the Lord added to their community
those destined to be saved.

—Acts 2:42–47

Simplicity of Life

There is a form of material poverty which is blessed.

"Ah, yes; we were poor, but happy."

Saint Francis fell in love with it.

In its more striking forms, it may look like a spare and bare existence. But this is not a material deprivation which dehumanizes. It humanizes us.

Simplicity of life is concerned with our relationship to things. But the heart of its meaning is the relatedness of persons. It is positive and blessed because it is grounded in the right order of valuing persons over objects.

Things are good. They are better and best when they are for persons, personal existence, personal celebration.

Life is for people: hence, simplicity.

We travel light enough so that the goods of the earth may be enjoyed and celebrated by all, so that they may bring glory to God. We travel light enough so that we ourselves may be for persons, rather than expend our lives collecting, maintaining, and replacing objects.

In simplicity, we are empowered to see the destitute, to share of our abundance, to ease the dehumanizing poverty that cries out to us. It enables us to give freely, to be more equitable. It frees us to engage the injustices of the world which are often the source of personal degradation. It makes us less fearful to put our security at risk.

In simplicity, we are given time to enter the grace of our human poverty. If we do not surround and suffocate ourselves with things, by which we manage and control our lives, we are far less likely to believe in the illusion that we have no need of God. We would less likely pretend that we are "self-made" men and women. Simplicity, as a liberation from the chains of consumerism, is also a call to prayer, wherein we encounter our spiritual poverty before God and discover the joy of recognizing ourselves as loved and forgiven creatures. Simplicity, moreover, gives us time for each other, for relationships and intimacy and friendship. A simple change in our style of working, consuming, or spending time with television profoundly affects our availability for persons.

Simplicity is as related to love as it is to justice.

It is freedom from compulsive addictions and entrenched escape mechanisms.

It is liberty to see ourselves anew and to disengage from the comforts that blind us to the face of the poor.

It unfetters us, that we might play and savor the moment, that we might give thanks and sing appreciation.

It can unlock us, finally, that we might do bold things, that we might more fully be men and women, not for things, but for others.

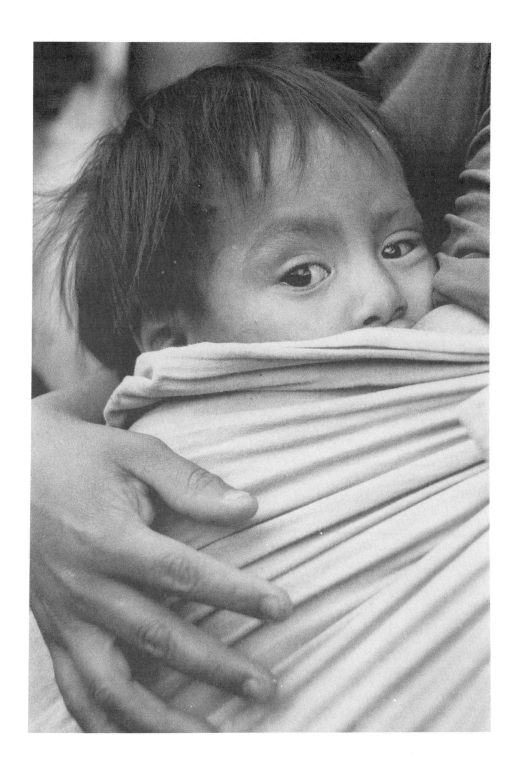

Twelve Steps

We buried Father Joe Collins today. He was a Jesuit Priest Alcoholic. Simple as that.

He would have liked me to say it that directly. In fact, his own words—which he wanted me to write some day—were even more direct.

"My name is Joe. I'm a drunk, a junkie, a terminal neurotic. Of course, I happen to be a Christian, a Catholic, a religious, a priest. But let us not put the cart before the horse. I am an addict by nature, by temperament, by destiny. All these other things are accretions, adventitious, strictly gratuitous. Here I am, well over seventy, barely able to walk, generally decrepit. Several doctors have told me I should have died years ago. But here I am, wondering—with Alfie—'what's it all about?' More precisely, I'm asking myself: did it have to be this way? Did my order have to send me to eight treatment centers? Did they have to, with extreme generosity, pay exorbitant rates to keep me in 'lower Siberia' for five years? Had my 'problem' been nipped in the bud, would it have all been different?

"Alcoholism—along with its fellow addictions—is by far the most rapacious, destructive disease that afflicts any community, familial or religious."

And so he would write about alcoholism. But I want to write about him.

There were three redemptive groups in Father Collins' life: the Jesuits, AA, and lay communities. Out from under the weight of the bottle, he found freedom in them all.

It's hard to tell sometimes whether the Jesuit order is a brotherhood, a motherhood, or a family; but in the case of Joe, it was a little bit of all. In some ways, we shared the longest and sharpest pains with him; and as he says above, this group which St. Ignatius called the "least society" was true to him in good times and in bad, in sickness and in health. His life in the Jesuits showed how fragile a big brotherhood could be—and how powerless, at times, to help those who are closest. But his brothers did not run from it; and how dear to Saint Ignatius they must be for it.

Alcoholics Anonymous did more for him in concrete and simple ways, especially in the later years of his life. It energized his spirituality, provided support through some of the most harrowing sieges, and sparked a mission in him that is read out in pages and pages of his personal testimonial. He probably felt most secure and accepted there, because it was here that he found people who *knew*, who did not "take offense," as he would put it.

But then there were the lay communities—who gave Joseph Collins something that neither the Jesuits nor AA could give.

They let him be their priest, even when he could not sport degrees or spout dogmas, even when he was unkempt and ecclesiastically disorderly-looking, even when he could not hold down a job, even when he could offer them little more than another grand unrealizable plan, even when he did not think very much of himself at all. They welcomed him—and the Christ he carried in his unfinished hopes, his pocketful of projects, and his restless concern for the downtrodden.

More, they cherished the sacrament he could bring.

These young friends kept him a priest. They probably kept him alive and kept him Joe, too.

And this, perhaps, is the most amazing thing about his life. Indeed, he had the graces of priesthood and Jesuit brotherhood and he had the redeeming comradeship of Alcoholics Anonymous. But what was most striking to me was that among those friends of Father Joe Collins, a man who said such seemingly harsh things about himself in the long paragraph that began this article, you would find the finest, loveliest of humans in all the world.

And they loved him.

And he knew it, too.

Television and Time

"Time," concludes pollster Louis Harris, who has charted America's loss of it, "may have become the most precious commodity in the land. . . ."

Most seriously, this shortcut society is changing the way the family functions. Nowhere is the course of the rat race more arduous, for example, than around the kitchen table. Hallmark, that unerring almanac of American mores, now markets greeting cards for parents to tuck under the Cheerios in the morning. ("Have a super day at school," chirps one card) or under the pillow at night ("I wish I were there to tuck you in"). . . .

Why do we work so hard? Why do we have so little time to spare? What does this do to us and our children? And what would we give up in order to live a little more peaceably?

—*Time*, April 24, 1989

I had given a talk in a "poor white" part of a midwestern city. I spoke of the media, and how we so easily come to be possessed by these strange possessions.

A man approached me after the presentation, a bit defensive but friendly, and remarked that I was against the very thing that his kids loved most. And why did I want to deprive them of that?

It was television. They lived in a flat, there were no parks around, the streets were not very inviting; and their one respite was television.

I asked him how much they watched.

"Well, on Saturday, they get up about six to start with the cartoons . . . and they watch until the end of Saturday Night Live."

How could I tell him that I was not the enemy, that I was not against his

kids or their enjoyments? How could I explain that the whole issue was life?
What is life for? What is time for?

The range of estimates for weekly time expenditures has averaged out,
over a number of studies, into the following categories:
• 56 hours a week sleeping;
• 40 hours a week working (highly flexible according to age, what "counts"
as work, and the fact that a sizable minority of breadwinners have employ-
ment combinations that total well over 40 hours);
• 30 hours a week watching T.V.;
• 20 hours a week listening to the radio;
• 18 hours a week eating;
• 8.5 hours a week reading (the most widely "read" weekly material in
this nation is *T.V. Guide*);
• 4 hours a week: other.

If this is anywhere near accurate, it seems we spend about 13 or 14 years
of our lives watching television — giving it more time over the long range
than any other conscious activity. At prime-time rates, we might spend — if
we live to the ripe age of 75 — three uninterrupted years of our lives watching
commercials.

The *Wall Street Journal* has called our affliction a "Time Famine." As
opposed to those countries which do not have enough to consume for the
bare living of life, we find ourselves consuming so much, we have no time
to live.

So the question emerges: what did those people of the 1940s, before
television, do with those extra 13 years of their lives?
There was a popular song when I was very young. It went, "The moon
belongs to everyone, the best things in life are free."

In the joyless economy of consumerism and the fascination for objects,
have we been convinced that those "best things in life," if free, must be
valueless?
What are the "other activities" we are allowed to enjoy for those last

remaining "four" hours of the week when we are not sleeping, consuming, producing or watching?

Solitude, nature, prayer, intimacy, relationship, visiting, being.

Such experiences we hunger for.
Such are the conditions of our "famine."

Freedom To Lose

The experience I had on arriving in Tulsa was strangely similar to that of other times and places. It might be a woman advertising executive in Detroit, a Texas lawyer, a university dean in New Orleans.

Here it was an Oklahoma oil man.

I'm always struck how such people find time to pick up a stranger who is coming to their diocese or university or parish to speak. And yet, somehow we never seem strangers.

The man in Tulsa seemed like a kindred spirit from the start. He had even gone to Rockhurst College (where I had once taught philosophy) before joining the Marines and then coming back to the States to get in the oil business. Perhaps it was when he told me he was a religiously "conservative" Catholic and politically something of a radical.

Anyway, I was stunned again. How does our God continue to manage to raise up such startling people of faith and service? Already, although this was to be a tiring weekend, I felt renewed riding along with him to the parish rectory.

It turns out, talking to the staff and some of the people in this liturgically and politically vital parish, that the man who picked me up had been very, very wealthy. Apparently he lost it all when the oil market deflated in the eighties.

Actually, he had told me this on the highway. Stunned in 1981, battered in 1986, the company he owned had gone bankrupt. Worse, he had personally guaranteed the company loans.

I was told that before the financial setback, he and his family were uncommonly generous. A parish in a poor part of town would be in financial straits; they would find a gift check for $10,000. A young businessperson would be trying to get a start; he would be generously staked. A book on spirituality and peace would inspire the man; a copy would be given to every member of the parish.

I'm sure there was much more. I'm equally sure that most of it had to stop after the mid-1980s; even though, like so many others who are astute at organization, business and imagination, he was able to rebuild things anew.

But he had told me during our car-ride "Since that Chapter II filing for bankruptcy, I've felt so much freer and happier." (A priest-friend of his maintained that such "freedom" was felt only because, long before the business difficulties, my friend was a man close to God.)

Even though I may not meet him again, I think I will always remember this man I met so briefly—whether in the image of him wondering at the airport if I, with my grey hair, could be the one in the picture, or sitting with his wife and three children at the 9:30 Sunday Mass, or talking with me about his favorite books and quiet dreams.

Although an uncommonly fine American, there are many like him. There are other men and women of astute business sense and organizational skill as well as profound spiritual sense and moral courage. They hunger for more than the ideology of greed and self-inflation can offer. They deserve more than pious warnings about the dangers of selfish capitalism. They are large of heart, and their imaginations search for ways to use their expertise and genius for others, for faith, and for the justice and service which is intrinsic to that faith.

In most cases, they have found ways to do it. They often have a life of prayer and are as unafraid of solitude as they are of social disapproval. They have in some way found community—either by covenant with other families or couples, through a local church, or especially through the firm commitment to a family life.

They have a passion for justice, which is neither knee-jerk liberalism nor reactive conservatism. They realize that their faith, if it is to have flesh and blood, must lead them to the poor. They know that their nation and government, while offering the most productive system in the history of the world and providing ample opportunity for them to build fortune and security, is also profoundly flawed in its myths of consumerism, nationalism and "self-made" pretension.

They enjoy the fruits of their labor in their homes, schools, and neighborhoods; and they are committed to finding ways to share these benefits with others. And another thing: they always seem to have found ways to let the marginal and the wounded speak to them.

When you meet one of them, you realize that there is more than one way to live a simple life.

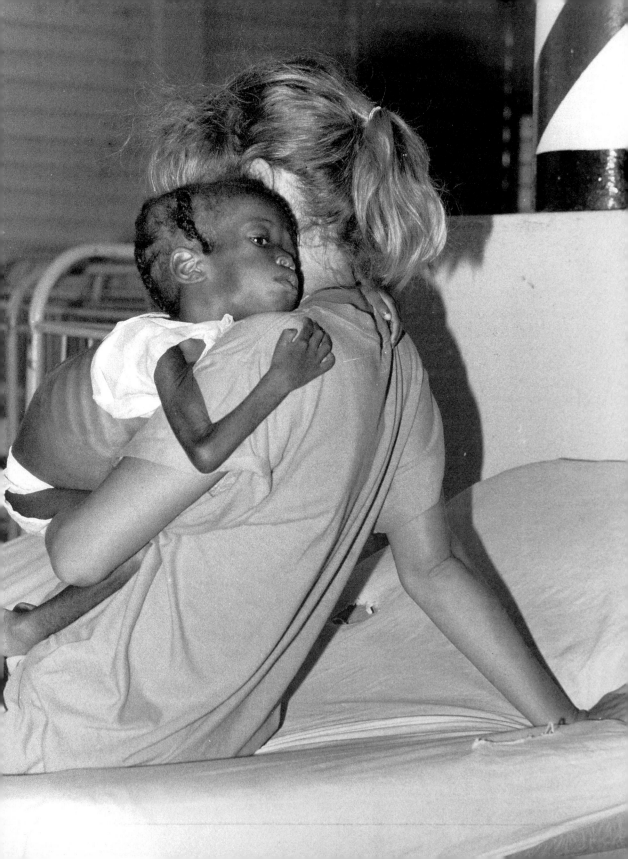

Liberty for Compassion

Give me your tired, your poor, your huddled masses
Yearning to breathe free.
The wretched refuse of your teeming shore.
Send these, the homeless, tempest-tossed to me.
I lift my lamp beside the golden door.

The words of Emma Lazarus on the Statue of Liberty have a special bitter-sweet paradoxical taste in these times. A case could be made that it is precisely the poor huddled masses, the wretched refuse of the earth, the homeless who are least welcome to our shores in this day and age.

Indeed, some of our national leaders stoke a smoldering terror at the prospect of teeming migrations from the South. There is a new self-righteous brittleness that is expressed in George Will's unblinking pronouncement that it was "not 'wretched refuse' but liberty-loving risk-takers" which the rest of the world bestowed on us.

Rather than be disheartened, however, at a selfishness that sometimes seems institutionalized, even sacramentalized in American culture, I am continually amazed by the grace and generosity of individuals. The yearning of the human spirit that was part of all those who came to this land will not, in the long run, be stifled by the closing of our shores and borders. Even if those who advise fear and retrenchment should win by some legislative or executive maneuver, even if public policy and mass consciousness be reduced to the celebration of arrogance and the deriding of compassion, there will always spring up from our people, I'm convinced, the compelling sentiment of Emma Lazarus. Even if we should shut our nation's boundaries to the poor, the poor will nonetheless call us to them, to a devotion of service, to a celebration of liberty.

Perhaps, more important than all indictments of materialism or enumer-
ations of the plight of the poor, what will be most freeing and liberating for
us in this country will be the discovery of our own internal liberty to love
and serve humanity by sharing our abundant land, technology, ingenuity and
yes—albeit sometimes hidden—generosity.

We have splendid people in this land. Especially among the young, those
who yet entertain the desires for uncommon service, there are remarkable
hearts and minds waiting only to be unlocked.

The journal entries of a group of high school students make it all so clear:
if we are willing to take the time and the risk to let go of the ordinary
securities protecting our experience, if we are willing to enter a world of
solidarity with others by the choices for simplicity and personal encounter
with "the poor," we discover a hitherto untapped freedom and compassion
within us.

The following are reflections from a group of young middle-class men
and women who had spent their Christmas and semester holidays—of all
things and in of all places—caring for poor children in Haiti.

The minute we walked in, we were greeted by outstretched arms of
little kids hoping to be picked up and played with. As I saw their
outstretched hands I was given the satisfaction of knowing that my
presence was valued and needed. Before I came, I had the doubt of
not knowing whether I could do any good. Yesterday I saw these kids
with bloated stomachs and diseases. I tried to avoid picking them up
and holding their hands because I was afraid of getting some disease.
But now, as I watch them smile and reach out for my hand, I don't
care what I catch. All I know is that from now on, the most important
thing is to give these kids a feeling of love and happiness.—Jim Dames

In a country of oppression and poverty I am amazed to see smiles, for
in a country of wealth and waste it's so typical to see a child crying for
not getting everything he wants. In Haiti they share everything, which
is practically nothing, while in America they share nothing and yet have
everything. God help them both.—Kelly Holloran

Now I know what misery is. It used to be just an image; now I know
it's real. I know I've changed and grown, and I'm not afraid of the
change in me. I welcome it. The experiences I've had will be with me

forever. And if I can live my life with more compassion for people, then I'm doing my part in the world.—Jennifer Kennedy

There is no way on earth for me to describe the poverty. They have as many as twelve people living in a hut about the size of my walk-in closet. I feel so guilty. I take so much for granted. I can get so mad at myself for having so much and not even taking time out to be thankful. I am so very blessed.—Julie James

He is blind in one eye and partially blind in the other. All he wanted to do was to be rocked or just held. After a while he fell asleep in my arms. I didn't want to put him down when we left.—Chris O'Leary

These are words of gifted young people abiding in a gifted land. They show that there is a Mother Teresa or Jean Vanier in each of us waiting for liberty. They show the enduring resilience of the human spirit that has been called forth from them by loving parents, caring teachers and, yes, the poor, the huddled masses yearning to breathe free.

Opening our hearts and shores to the people of whom Emma Lazarus wrote is a risk not only for the sake of "them." It is for the sake of our own deepest freedom.

I know how you know love. It's in the eyes. They express everything. Love, despair, pain, happiness—the joy to see someone you can hug. That's my goal, to find some child to hug every day. A desperate child who needs the love. I have the need to give. I never thought I could feel this way. The first day we were here, all I wanted to do was go home. Now I see the beauty in the love given.

The faces of the poor are seen by the eyes of simplicity.

Play

A hand. A ball. A wall.

Sometimes I think the world should work like the Forest Park Handball Club.

I try to get down there as often as I can — and I think it is as much for my spiritual and psychological welfare as for the exercise.

If you venture there during the week, you will often meet up with some of the older members of the 150-member club, and some of the newcomers as well.

Gratefully, if you are a middling player like myself, both in age and skills, you will probably be the "runner" — the left side player, who is supposed to cover most of the court and go deep for the return of long drives, which even people in their seventies can launch with clever suddenness.

On weekends, the strongest players come out, some as early as nine-thirty in the morning; and a player of my meager caliber can sometimes wind up being a right-side partner to one of the best players in the state.

Any day, it's great. The sun and the park. The people. The challenge of a game at which you can still get better even if you are pushing fifty.

When I first went to the handball courts over fifteen years ago, I was rather shy — not only because of my abilities, but because I knew no one. But as time moved on, it became one of the most agreeable places I have found in the world.

It is truly a melting pot: Chinese and Irish, African and Jewish, Italian and German, American Indian and just plain old Saint Louisan in descent and ethnic background. I have never seen a possible partner excluded for ethnic or racial reasons. The rules of equity and skill govern all.

These people mourn their dead, they remember their great ones, they welcome the newcomer, they like to put on a dinner and dance once a year.

They have all occupations: painters and roofers, priests and high-schoolers, teachers and coaches, gravediggers and lawyers, judges and policemen, social workers and unemployed, grocery stockers and restaurant owners, politicians and drivers, cooks and preachers, professors and accountants. It's a great mix. You cannot visit the place without sensing the diversity of life. Fathers play with sons and daughters, priests with lapsed Catholics, politicians with protesters.

What is this mystery of play, of the open air, of exercise? Why is it so easy to enjoy the sky and the moment, to relish the expenditure of energy and the fatigue of body? Why is it so simple? Why is play so profound? How is it so real?

Perhaps it is in the fact that there is a spirituality to handball, even an asceticism to it. The years of playing demand a pruning of egos. Weakness of character as well as strategy are revealed; but with the longstanding acceptance of one another—with the possible exception of obnoxious behavior which is always and immediately confronted—progress is gradually made. Change and deepening take place.

One also recognizes, after awhile, that there is an unnamed citadel within each player. There are great interior battles, the wounds of which are noticed over time. There are the mighty labors of family, job, and aging for which the game serves as respite and release. There is the bottom of the self that is sometimes only revealed—and then, only fleetingly—on the court.

One of the characters, "Bama," died recently. I used to wonder if the handball court was the place where he found his greatest acceptance—and even there it was sometimes a chancy proposition. But he loved coming there. He said he would be happy to die on the court some day.

Well, on one of those early spring days, when winter lets go of its grip, while leading in the second game 11-2, Bama leaned against the side of the handball court wall. And he got his wish.

Simple Gifts

Thanksgiving is my favorite American holiday. It seems to represent the best in us. Not only our heritage and traditions, but our future hope.

One who gives thanks is not like the Pharisee in Jesus' famous parable, who puffs that he is "not like the rest" of people — especially that publican — and pointedly observes that he has really done quite well for himself.

No, true thanksgiving is more the attitude of Mary's Magnificat, where she takes delight in her saving God, the God who has done wonders for her, the God of justice and preferential love for the poor.

Thanksgiving is not the time for making comparisons. It's the time for savoring the precious gift of life in whatever measure we may partake of it.

Thanksgiving is affirmation. It is appreciation. It is naming and blessing the good — of the world, of our nation, of each of us. And it automatically leads us to want to share those goods with others.

Thanksgiving is a corrective for all the cravings in us, the impatient unsettledness of not having it all, of not having enough, of not having more. It invites us to savor and cherish what is, what we are, and all those we love.

If we learn thanksgiving, we are less likely to take anything for granted and we are more likely to give the greatest of delights to God: our gratitude. Perhaps that is why Christ is always charmed by the thankfulness that cherishes his gifts and always disappointed by the deadening ingratitude which takes everything for granted.

A former student of mine once told me of a paralyzed woman she visited over a number of years. Each month the woman seemed to lose just a bit more of her powers. And the loss over a year would be dramatic. Yet the woman would always say, "I'm just so glad I can. . . ." And then she would name any little gift that was left to her: talk, roll over, scratch, whisper, read, think, pray, respond with only a meager nod. She was always just so glad. And my student received such strength from her.

The old woman knew the greatest gift of all God had given her. She was given the irreplaceable opportunity to do something each day that no one else in the world could do. And that is to speak her own "yes."

"I hope. I love. I believe. I thank you."

It is our "yes," each one uniquely uttered when we speak to each other and to God, when we reach out to share the life we have with others, when we heal just a little more of the wounds of the world—that is the preeminent gift God has bestowed on us, the utterly singular gift that we extend to the world.

We hope for joys. We often settle for labor. But there is something far more wonderful offered us.

The great Indian Bengali poet Tagore wrote,

> I slept and dreamt, that life was all joy.
> I awoke and saw, that life was but service.
> I served and understood, that service was joy.

Happy Simplicity

There are those moments.

We catch a glimmer of the joy.

It all feels lighter. The weight of craving passes. The urgency of need ebbs and we are lifted into the realm of freedom.

For most of us it is only fleeting. A sign of what might be or what is meant to be.

And if we keep our hearts open, we are led.

We feel less driven. Constraints are loosened. We have a bit more time: to walk and pray, to be with the beloved, to appreciate what is, to share what we have.

But there are also those among us who seem to abide in that very freedom. Something is unlocked in them. There is, for all their humanity and frailty, a limpid clarity. It is a drink of purest water to see them.

She is a lover. There seems no time left for her to collect. The days are given. She opens doors, her open heart a house to strangers. She glides her way through town to visit. She is a Catholic Worker. Her labor is faith. Her work is charity. She travels light through time, and somehow, forsaking all the approvals of high documentation, privileged profession, child or spouse, career or social consequence, she transforms every face she beholds.

They have taken the risks that others only dream of. Home and offspring have not closed them upon the nest. They venture boldly: Christmas with their family and like families in Central America, spring breaks in Haiti, summers spent in the hot labors of justice. Their lives are spare, but not spartan. There are vacancies in them, room for one another, for the poor, for the voiceless. They are not cluttered, neither in their homes nor in their souls. Some of them have launched into downward mobility and they often sail. These couples have time, since they have learned not to hoard it. Their love is both courageous and opportune, since they have realized that love itself is the most renewable of natural and supernatural resources.

He is a president of a university and his room is a citadel. There is little other in it than the present, than presence. He is one of us who had yearned to give it all away long ago; and he never learned how to take it back bit by bit. When he is here, he is fully here. There seems to be no other acquisition on the agenda. He moves gracefully, unencumbered by the eighty years and the endless wants.

She is a doctor and a Sister. A villager who finally accepts a jeep for the sake of the people who might be reached, touched, healed. She lives by the sun and the stars. It is all very un-complex—in the midst of the terrible war around, the helicopters overhead, the future uncertain. She lets go of loves and labors, but they never leave her. She is so distant but so immediate.

They shine for us. They illumine our lives.
And, in our own fleeting moments of lightness, we feel closer to them than we had ever dared to imagine.

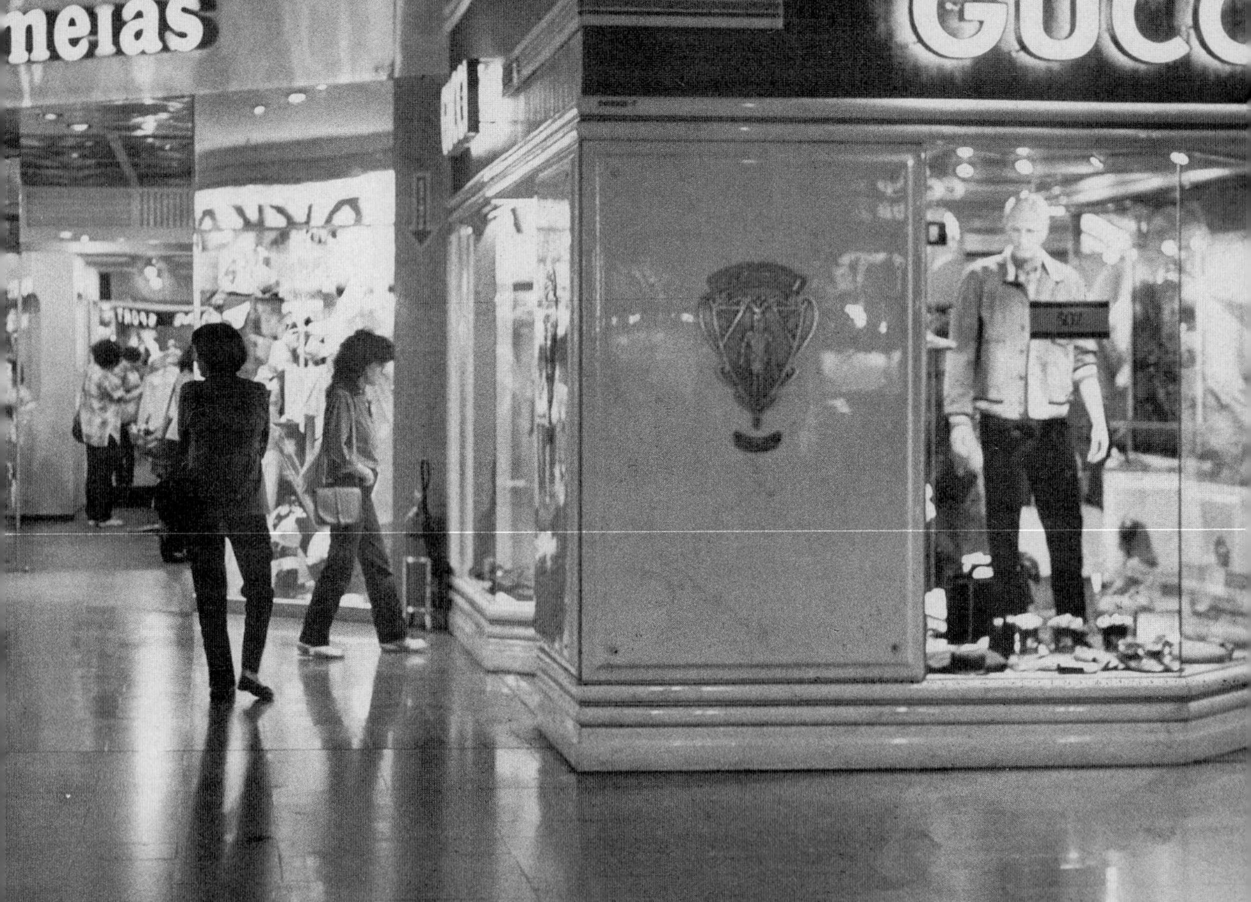
meias
GUCC

Time and Fortune

THE MONEY SOCIETY

Money, Money, Money is the incantation of today. Bewitched by an epidemic of money enchantment, Americans in the Eighties wriggle in a St. Vitus's dance of materialism . . . Under the blazing sun of money, all other values shine palely. . . .

An overwhelming 93% of recently surveyed teenage girls deemed shopping their favorite pastime, way ahead of sixth-rated dating. Back in 1967, around 40% of U.S. college freshmen told pollsters that it was important to them to be very well-off financially, as against around 80% who listed developing a meaningful philosophy of life as an important objective. But by 1986 the numbers had reversed. . . .

Says historian Mary Klein, ours is "an age where traditional self-identities are under great attack and great strain just from the pace of change. In that situation, money becomes a way of defining who you are by what you have."

—Fortune, July 6, 1987

FLASHY SYMBOL OF AN ACQUISITIVE AGE

One man who knows Trump well does see a rhyme and reason. Trump is a brilliant dealmaker with almost no sense of his own emotions or his own identity, this man says. He is a kind of black hole in space, which cannot be filled no matter what Trump does. Looking toward the future, this associate forsees Trump building bigger and bigger projects in his attempts to fill the hole but finally ending, like Howard Hughes, a multibillionaire living all alone in one room.

—Time, January 16, 1989

III

DEHUMANIZING
SPIRITUAL POVERTY

I know all about you;
how you are neither cold nor hot.
I wish you were one or the other,
but since you are neither, but only lukewarm,
I will spit you out of my mouth.

You say to yourself
    "I am rich
    I have made a fortune
    I have everything I want,"
never realizing that you are wretchedly
and pitiably poor and blind and naked too.

I warn you, buy from me the gold that has been tested in the fire
    to make you really rich and white robes to clothe you and cover
    your shameful nakedness and eye ointment to put on your eyes
    so that you are able to see. I am the one who reproves and
    disciplines those who are loved, so repent in real earnest.

Look, I am standing at the door, knocking.
If one of you hears me calling and opens the door,
I will come in to share your meal,
side by side with you.

—Revelation 3:15–22

The Poverty of Sin

The condition of sin is one of misery.

It is found in lovelessness or in the false material and spiritual riches which we cling to but which never satisfy us.

"My students are my poor, even though they come from wealthy families. There is addiction, abuse, neglect, a desperate loneliness."

"My rich associates, our board of directors, are all poor spiritually. I don't have to go out to a soup kitchen to find poverty."

"My community, even though well-off, has plenty of poverty that I can minister to."

The reality that people are referring to here is actually often our poverty-as-humans that every person in every condition has to face: we are all human and frail (a fact that the powerful or wealthy or spiritually adept may try to cover up, yet nonetheless experience).

But often enough, there is something else going on. It is not just our "being human." It is our flight from it. It is our disgust at it.

And such disgust, such evasion, such negation is what sin is all about.

The fact that Christ was like us in all of our weakness and tempted in every way yet did not sin indicates what sin actually is.

It is the rejection of being human. He alone was "truly Human" as well as "truly God."

In its extreme form, one can call this a "Howard Hughes kind of poverty," wherein a person has everything material but lives in constant dread and avoidance of human vulnerability. It is said that Hughes could not bear the touch of another person's skin during his last years. One would have to use paper towels to pass him food, never touching him or his sustenance. He consumed massive amounts of drugs to deaden the pain. And he was so afraid to lose, to let go of any particle of his being that he collected his own urine in gallon bottles.

The poor man.

And yet there is Howard Hughes in all of us, inhabiting all of our ruses, escapes, and pretense. In all our terror at the unmanageability of human existence, in all our destructiveness, in all our despair, in all our rage.

Clearly such a person needs the ministry of the word and sacrament of God—as each of us does. What is more, such a person is called.

"I came to call sinners."

If we acknowledge this poverty, not only in the world, but in our hearts, the call will inevitably be given.

But we run from confessing this deadly spiritual poverty, just as we run from the life-giving spiritual poverty of our human creatureliness. In fact, the flights are one and the same.

This face of poverty lurks in the cultures of death and the impulses of revenge. It inhabits the false securities which eventually possess us. It hides in our refusals to repent as a nation, or confess as a church or ask forgiveness as persons. It thrives in the degradation of women and the devaluation of children. It walks death row and the state house.

This poverty, too, must be named and embraced. So named, so faced, it will no longer hold us in its thrall.

Once again the Gospel is good news to the poor and sets the downtrodden free.

Revenge and Faith

When I was in grade school, our neighborhood was victimized by a bully. It wasn't very serious, but most kids were afraid of him and couldn't stand it when he was around. When he beat up on one friend of mine, I remember I went home and wondered if it would be possible to sabotage the bully someday or if I might be able to get strong enough to beat him up. It became clear, however, that if I just sabotaged him, he might track me down to get even with me; and that if I were strong enough to beat him up, he might later come back at me with some of his roughneck friends.

It was then that I thought that the only way to stop him was to kill him. I didn't try it.

When I was older, as a priest living in a small community on the North Side of Saint Louis, we were robbed at shotgun point by three creeps who chose the one day when my family was visiting us for supper. They took our coats, some money, a broken-down T.V. set, and the rings from our fingers (including my mother's engagement and wedding rings—worth more as remembrance than investment, I'm sure). I can still taste the rage, the sense of violation and the hostility I felt for anyone walking the streets who may have remotely resembled the culprits. And these people didn't even physically harm us.

So out of nowhere came Bernhard Goetz, the Manhattan Subway Vigilante, who seems to be the hero of a lot of people. He triggers the ache for vengeance in me which was first moved by the neighborhood bully. He also pulls and picks at the rage that I thought might have left me a year or so after the robbery. He makes the same kind of perverse sense that even Charles Bronson or Clint Eastwood make to me when I see one of their films.

The problem is, everything that appeals to me about this vigilante, about vengeance, about Bronson and Eastwood, is radically opposed to Christ.

I'm not saying that we by nature should be repulsed by vengeance — any more than any of us would by nature want to be honest or chaste or generous. I'm just saying that almost every word I have read or heard uttered about the "subway vigilante" comes out of the evil spirit, the spirit of darkness, the domain of sin. Our deepest problem here is that we are romanticizing the cleansing power of hatred.

"Try and take my money away. Make my day."

"I wish he could have killed all four of them."

"Next time they'll think twice if they know that a victim will be carrying an 'equalizer.' "

"It's something we'd all like to do. We'd all like to think that we would react the way Goetz did."

Indeed, it is not a new conclusion about human nature that, in essence, we all would like to have unlimited power, unlimited pleasure, and unlimited possessions. There are some people, to be sure, who think that the only "realistic" way to get through this life is by the exercise of force, manipulation, deceit and extortion. There are others who think that only power and might can insure our protection, that guns alone are our rock of safety, our stronghold, our only security which merits trust.

But is this the truth? Is this the way God has actually made us? Is this the promise to which God calls us? Is this what Christ commands us?

The question is easily answered, although not easily accepted. We have a God who has made a new creation out of us, in Jesus Christ. We have a new heroism. And it is not the heroism of Captain Marvel, the Lone Ranger, John Wayne, Rocky II, Charles Bronson, or poor Bernhard Goetz.

It is the heroism of Jesus.

We may not like this, but that's the way it is if we say that we are followers of Christ.

Does this mean that Goetz will be condemned by God? I doubt it. But that is only because I know that the God I worship is not the stuff of childhood fantasies of vengeance or the fabrication of all the violated and enraged victims of history. And this is a source of consolation to me.

After all, if God is best represented by the actions of Goetz or the words of talk-show callers, I know that I myself wouldn't really have much of a chance.

I'll stick with the God that Jesus made flesh.

The Problem of Riches

We find great resistance — especially in our affluent culture — to any religious challenge which focuses upon our economic system and our way of life. We resist the truth of the gospels.

But what of Christ himself? How might a nation which often calls itself Christian respond to his words on wealth and poverty? Dare bishops or preachers "stick to religious issues" of faith and really teach as Jesus taught?

One wonders.

Many people would be upset — and not just businesspersons. There is no doubt that the clear, persistent, and challenging words of Jesus concerning money would find all of us (especially, one might think, bishops, priests, and people in religious life) confounded by the distance between the commands of Christ and the conduct of our lives. Would we even tolerate him in our pulpits?

> Do not store up treasures for yourselves on earth, where moths and woodworms destroy them and thieves can break in and steal. But store up treasures for yourselves in heaven where neither moth nor woodworms destroy them and thieves cannot break in and steal. For where your treasure is, there will your heart be also. (Mt. 6:19-21)

> No one can be the slave of two masters; you will either hate the first and love the second, or treat the first with scorn. You cannot be the slave both of God and money. (Mt. 6:24)

> I tell you solemnly, it will be hard for a rich person to enter the kingdom of heaven. Yes, I tell you again, it is easier for a camel to pass through the eye of a needle than for a rich person to enter the kingdom of heaven. (Mt. 19:21-24)

Alas for you, scribes and Pharisees, you hypocrites! You who pay your tithe of mint and dill and cummin and have neglected the weightier matters of the Law—justice, mercy, good faith. These you should have practiced, without neglecting the others. You blind guides, straining out gnats and swallowing camels. (Mt. 23:23)

I tell you solemnly, this poor widow has put more in than all who have contributed to the treasury, for they have all put in money they had over, but she from the little she had has put in everything she possessed, all she had to live on. (Mk. 12:44)

How happy are you who are poor: yours is the kingdom of God . . . But alas for you who are rich: you are having your consolation now. (Lk. 6:21, 24)

But God said to him, "Fool! This very night the demand will be made for your soul; and this hoard of yours, whose will it be then?" So it is when you store up treasure for yourself in place of making yourself rich in the sight of God. (Lk. 12:20-1)

None of you can be my disciple unless you give up all your possessions. (Lk. 14:33)

There was a rich man who used to dress in finery and feast magnificently every day. And at his gate there lay a poor man called Lazarus. . . . (Lk. 17: 19-31)

"There is still one thing you lack. Sell all that you own and distribute the money to the poor and you will have treasure in heaven; then come, follow me." But the young person, hearing this, was filled with sadness, for he was very rich. (Lk. 18:23)

These are strong words. And it is good to remember that it is indeed Christ, and not our own virtue, which will save us. And it is also good to remember that Jesus loved Bethany, enjoyed the celebrations of life, was delighted at the ointment that eased his tired feet. He was not against the good things of the earth because he knew they were for the glory of God and the help of souls.

Zacchaeus was a rich man whom Jesus met. What did Jesus say to him?

Not "I reject you," or "Woe to you," but "I want to go to your home today."

And Zacchaeus, so struck by the open heart of the One who called him, said that half of his holdings would go to the poor.

And Jesus Christ did not say: "Only half?"

Yet—and it would do well for us to consider this—he was betrayed for thirty pieces of silver by a person who pretended to have a concern for the poor.

Judas's concern, we know, was not for the poor.

It was for himself.

Lent

The themes of repentance, reform, and the acknowledgement of sin, all so prominent in the lenten liturgies, bring to mind a sermon I once gave on the Last Judgment.

Rather than formulate my own idea of what the final accounting might be like, I decided to restrict myself to Christ's own presentation — that which can be found in the twenty-fifth chapter of St. Matthew's Gospel.

Consequently, the homily was about food for the hungry, hospitality for the homeless, clothing for the naked, and visiting the imprisoned.

Jesus seemed to think that these things were so important that he not only identified himself with the least fortunate human being, but he quite clearly claimed that the very fire of hell would be the result of neglecting the works of love, service, and ministry to the least human person. For Christians, then, it was not a matter of liberalism or socialism that the poor be housed, clothed, fed, and visited; it was a matter of faith.

I remember a man, quite upset, approaching me to ask, "When are you priests going to stop talking about this love stuff and start talking about the real things you are supposed to talk about — like sin and the threat of eternal damnation?"

Well, I had thought that was exactly the topic I had been talking about, so I asked him what sins he might be interested in hearing about and what hell he might have in mind. Clearly the sins I mentioned and the prospect of eternal loss presented by Jesus did not seem to be the "real stuff" for him.

We're all a little like this man. Sometimes it seems that we just don't want to hear about the truth of our own sinfulness, even when we are protesting loudly that this is what we want. What we really desire is to hear about the sins of other people — those people making "a mess of their lives," those people "out there," those characters who are doing all those bad things that we ourselves would never think of doing.

Thus, self-righteous people who are secure in their sense of virtue want to hear indictments of loose living, fornication and the tepid treachery of heterodoxy.

Fornicators, meanwhile, would be pleased to hear of the sins of the self-righteous.

We do not like to hear about our own sinfulness, our own need for repentance, our own urgent need to reform. When we say "tell us about sin and punishment," we are not requesting a sermon dealing with our own moral failures. In fact, we will often resist such a sermon with all our might.

We will complain that popes and bishops are being too political and too concerned with economics and war if our sinful inclinations are toward economic, militaristic, and national pride.

Or, we will say that popes and bishops should not talk of sexuality, abortion, and family life—if our moral compromises are more domestic and intimate.

(And even here—at this comparison, some of us will bristle: "But you can't compare money and nationalism with the *real* sins of sex." Or, "But you can't compare little sexual peccadillos like infidelity or self-indulgence with the *real* moral failures of injustice.")

Could clerics admit to the damage that clerics have done, not only by scandal, but by the misrepresentations of Christ's message and salvation? Could conservatives finally be as adept at naming their own idols as they are at pointing out those of others? Could liberals be willing to criticize themselves as wholeheartedly and passionately as they do the Pope?

Ah, the paradoxes of repentance. How difficult it is for me to acknowledge my own sin, how easy it is to project it on others. How subtle are our own resistances to conversion.

Thus, poor Dives appears every Lent for our benefit. There he is in hell and he is asking for the favor of having someone warn his own kin about the fate of those who neglect the poor. And he is told simply this: Your kin had Moses and the prophets and didn't believe; they won't believe even someone who could rise from the dead.

How knowledgeable Jesus was of our condition. He did rise from the dead. And we still ignore his message. "Speak to us of sins, but not our own. Tell us of some hell, but not our own."

And like so many of those unfortunate souls of the gospels—for the most part self-assured people, those who thought that they were so good and pure, those who were always condemning the marginal, the unclean, the unorthodox, the unacceptable, those who could not muster as much compassion as they could superciliousness, those who fretted that Christ was too lenient and forgiving, those who, like a withered vine could bear no fruit because they could not bear repentance—we poor benighted ones can so sadly lose it all.

If we repress the invitation to reform we cannot hear the message of redemption. And we will not bear the fruit of faith, which is love.

Idols

I had never been comfortable with the topic of sin in retreats.

I got it behind me.

In eight-day retreats, it would come on the second or third day and I would get it over with.

Make the slate clean.

Get it straightened out.

A general confession served.

But on my first directed retreat, the director didn't want to get it over with. He didn't even want to get into it. He wanted me to work the full eight days.

Perhaps he knew that I would always stop after sin. I'd get it out of the way and then not know what to do for the following days.

It was all clear. Settled. Secure.

And so, we were six days into the retreat. I thought sin had passed. We were on to other things.

Yet the director kept giving me readings that reminded me of sin.

There were five meditations on the sixth day. They seemed all to be concerned with sin.

And I had my fill of it.

Philosophers came back to haunt me. Feuerbach, Nietzsche, Sartre.

What was the meaning of this self-flagellation in sin-consciousness?

Why does God want us to wallow in this self-construed miasma called sin?

I hated the very thought of it.

It was the fourth hour of prayer and sin hounded me.

Yet I had made amends. I had made it all right. I was free and clear. Why did it not pass and leave me be—to spend the next paltry two days waiting for the end, waiting to get back to work again?

I felt a nausea—the experience that the great commentators called "spiritual repugnance." But this was real nausea. I was sick and tired. Sick and tired of the probe, of the scavenging for sin to be ashamed of. I could not even read a word of my favorite theologian or spiritual writer.

Perhaps the philosophers were right. God is a degradation of the human spirit. Sartre had written: "If God exists, humanity is nothing; if humanity exists, God is. . . ."

And so, I thought, I was losing my faith.

An old solution came to me. It was a prayer that had carried me through numerous dark nights. "Oh God, you know me and you love me."

But the uttering of it only made me sicker and more tired. It just didn't do the tricks it had done in the past.

Then the invitation came: John, say, "God, you know me and you love me; and it is not because of anything I have ever done or accomplished."

I could not get beyond the first eight words.

I detested the implications. If what I have ever done or accomplished does not even make a difference, then why have I done it? Why not have an affair? Why not kill if I want? Why not vegetate in front of a T.V. for the rest of my life? But I had *not* done these things. I had worked hard. Was that for nothing? I tried hard. Was that worthless?

But the invitation persisted . . . "and it is not because of anything I have ever done or accomplished. . . ."

I resisted for over an hour.

And then I gave in.

"God, you know me and you love me, and it is not because of anything I have ever done or accomplished."

Somehow in that moment I knew sin as I had never known before. I felt like a ball of sin. I saw the face of Hitler within me. In so seemingly insignificant a moment, I saw murder and even hate.

And yet, some terrible burden seemed lifted. Some awesome truth seemed named. And, naked in that truth, I felt loved as I had never felt before.

What is it that we worship? Pleasure? Power? Satisfaction? Escape?
These are the easy idols to name, for many of us.
But what if we worship our own actions, our virtue, our labors, the products of our hands and will?
If these are called into question, does it seem that the walls of faith itself may be tumbling down?

I thought if I had ever admitted that my own efforts were in some way inconsequential to the reality of God, I would stop. I would give up all efforts.

But that was only if I must persist in worshipping my own effort.
Saint Paul once said that he finally counted his efforts as worthless trash. And then, in a moment's breath, he sang of the great race — now run not out of fear, but sheer joy.

The following year, I continued to run my race. But for the first time, the running was less in fear and — indubitably — more in joy.

Women Things

In China you are allowed to have one child. Unless you have the misfortune of giving birth to a girl. You may try again. Once.

In Bombay it has been reported that the abortions performed at clinics which provide sex-prognostications run 97% female fetuses aborted; 3% male.

In parts of South America, a woman goes into mourning if her first child is a baby girl.

In Southern Africa it is not uncommon that men beat their wives with the command: "I paid for you; now do what I want."

And in the United States, a young Catholic high school senior publicly responds to a presentation on sexism in the media with the observation, "What are you so upset about? Men have always used women to make money."

Why do we deny the sin of sexism?

Is it because we deny sin itself?

Injustice to women, like every injustice in world history, is a tactic that reduces humans to the status of objects. We render the other faceless, voiceless, selfless.

Yet women do injustices to themselves, do they not? They have their own problem with "otherness."

Some women think there is no problem with sexism. Others think it is the only problem.

Some women perceive exclusion from ordained ministry and exclusive liturgical language as instances of injustice. Other women see those who raise these issues as uppity dissidents. Rarely do they talk with, rarely do they look at, each other.

In all the great diversity of the church, and not in this issue alone, there is one constant: an unwillingness to hear or see the other. The other has no face, no voice, no reality. The other cannot be heard or seen. Liberal feminists cannot speak with conservative traditionalists. The traditionalist blinds herself to the face of the dissident.

The enthroned ego insists that it be so.

Sexism, at bottom, is not about sex. It is hatred of otherness. This is not an attribute unique to males — although men for the most part have institutionalized it in their own favor. It is, rather, a tendency that eats at the roots of our being.

The refusal to see the face of the other, to hear the voice of the other, is the prime instance of sin.

So, "Who says sexism is a sin?"

Well, we may not like the word, but the reality it stands for is undeniable. In fact, if we are willing to search the terrain of human sinfulness over the regions of vanity, greed, lust, pride, or hatred, the relationship between men and women will be found haunting our every step. In each of these sins, rejection of and domination over the other is at the core. And in most cultures, the domination and rejection is that of men over women.

The most insistent and ancient example of "otherness" is the other sex. Nation and color are strong, but sex is foundational. And the primal war of control is waged in the arena of gender.

If sexism is denied, it is sin which is really repressed. And the debilitating poverty of lovelessness — hatred of the other in its most radical expression — is lost to us.

We cling to the prison of ego and declare ourselves free.

Death Row

Gerald Smith was still alive on Missouri's Death Row. For a while he wanted to be killed. And perhaps, at that time, never had so many decent people agreed with the wishes of the criminal mind. They wanted him finished.

For the meantime, these wishes went unfulfilled.

But George "Tiny" Mercer, convicted for a brutal rape and murder in 1978, made up for it. He was executed in the early moments of 1989.

The talk shows crackled with words like "scum" and "animal"—one caller maintaining that "there are some people that have no good in them at all." Many of these callers identified themselves as Christians, although it may be difficult to associate their sentiments with the teachings of the Lord whose name their religion bears.

Scriptural justifications are sometimes offered, but never from the gospels. At best, we are given passages from Leviticus or Numbers to justify a Christian stance. One phrase was repeated which I had heard once in response to a talk on the sanctity of human life: "But even Jesus himself said, 'an eye for an eye, a tooth for a tooth.' "

So distant have we veered from the teachings of Jesus that we use his very words to refute his intent. If we care enough to examine the Gospel of Matthew, we find he was actually negating the statement which our phone-caller was attributing to him.

It is understandable that some people see fit to eliminate others: especially the relatives of an innocent person who has been violated or murdered by a brutal killer. In this context, rejection of the death penalty is seen by some as a callousness toward the victim. "Why so much sympathy for the criminal, and so little for the victims?" But the issue is never whether the pain or loss of the victim was devastating. It is, rather, what does one do with the criminal left in our midst?

There may indeed be very good secular reasons to execute a criminal, good utilitarian reasons, good financial ones, possibly even good psychological ones. But if one has any aspiration at all to live in the truth of Jesus Christ, the reasons for execution cannot be found.

When one looks at the reality of Jesus, his life, teaching, and the redemption he brought us, there is no way to justify capital punishment. To be sure, Christ's cherishing of human life is not the only thing which is rejected in our appeals to "realism," and our derision of "do-goodism," "bleeding hearts," and "turn-the-other-cheekers." The fact is, Jesus was a bleeding heart who went about doing good and who advised us to turn the other cheek.

He certainly called a sin a sin, challenged sinners, and indicted those who harmed others. But he commanded us to forgive seventy-times-seven, not to return evil for evil and — if we would aspire to heaven — to treat the least of our brothers and sisters as we would treat him. Including those in prison.

And he was not talking about the "innocent." Innocence, as a matter of fact, has little or nothing to do with the value of a human life. If innocence were the issue, who among us would have value?

What is of issue is that each of us is made in the image of God and recreated in Jesus — even though we are sinners. The cup of Communion is the Blood of Christ, shed so that sins may be forgiven.

We make a mockery of Jesus and the Eucharist if we take innocence as our founding value for life. Our value is in the fact that God loves us and has died for us. The more we give ourselves to this truth, the more we "un-innocent" ones take part in the life of God.

The great sadness in the fact that a Christian nation calls for more executions is this: If our whole world were made up of people as guilty as Gerald Smith, Tiny Mercer — or supply any other notorious name — we, in our wisdom, would execute them all.

Jesus would have died for them.

War

Peace.

Everybody wants peace. Give peace a chance.

But do we really?

To be a peacemaker is not easy. It is not easy to forgive even your friends and relatives, much less a real enemy.

We choke on it. Reconciliation. Asking forgiveness. Laying down our arms, our resentments, our angers.

"If I forgive them, they will walk all over me."

"I'll forgive them if they forgive me first."

"I'll forgive him if he asks forgiveness."

"I'll forgive her if she admits her mistake."

But lay down our arms? Disarm? Forgive?

It's the stuff of moral heroism.

As it is in our personal lives, so it is in the public world.

We all have reasons to make war.

We all have our reasons not to seek peace.

And so it was in my ethics class. I had offered the opinion that the real foundation for Christian peacemaking is our faith in Christ.

It is in our discipleship of him who did not return evil for evil.

It is in our following of one who asked us to forgive seventy-times-seven.

It is in our conviction that *he* is our security, our trust, our rock of safety, our way, our life.

It is in our belief that Jesus was serious when he said that "whatsoever you do to the least . . . you do to me."

Well, I had a conservative seminarian and a liberal seminarian in that class. And they did not like what I was saying.

The conservative—who seemed to have identified the way of Christ with the security of America said:

"You have to be realistic. If you try to disarm or seek peace with the Russians, they will walk all over you. Our only hope is that we have the bomb and that they are afraid to attack us. You can't 'turn the other cheek' with atheists like them. It just does not work to follow the gospel in this dog-eat-dog world."

On the other side of the room was the liberal seminarian. He said that he used to agree with my romantic pacifism, but that he had come to face the facts of poverty and oppression.

"You cannot instruct the poor to lay down the gun. Sometimes, for the oppressed, the gun is their only hope, their last resort. They cannot be expected to turn the other cheek when they are dealing with capitalist oppressors. It is just not realistic to ask them to be 'Christlike.' It doesn't work. Face the facts."

Well the fact was this, for all to see. Two Catholics—one liberal and one conservative—put their hope in the gun, rigid and ready, and its power to inflict violence.

The one thing these two Christians agreed on was this: Christ is not realistic; Christ is not relevant to war.

And that is why, even among those who bear the name "Christian," there is rarely peace in this world.

"Come Back"

Repeat. Do you read? Do you read?

Are you in trouble? How did you get in trouble? If you are in trouble, have you sought help? If you did, did help come? If it did, did you accept it? Are you out of trouble? What is the character of your consciousness? Are you conscious? Do you have a self? Do you know who you are? Do you know what you are doing? Do you love? Do you know how to love? Are you loved? Do you hate? Do you read me?

Come back. Repeat. Come back. Come back. Come back.

—Walker Percy
Lost in the Cosmos: The Last Self-Help Book

IV

HUMANIZING
SPIRITUAL POVERTY

For it is not as if we had a high priest
who was incapable of feeling our weakness with us;
but we have one who has been tempted
    in every way that we are,
though he is without sin. . . .

He can sympathize with those who are ignorant or uncertain
because he too lives in the limitations of weakness. . . .

During his life on earth, he offered up prayer and entreaty
aloud and in silent tears
to the one who had the power to save him out of death,
and he yielded so humbly
that his prayer was heard.
                              —*Hebrews 4:15,16; 5:2,7–8*

Vulnerability

We are not God.

We are not full, not complete, not finished, not secure, not self-sustaining, not self-insuring.

This lack is poverty, but a poverty which is blessed, pronounced good with all created being.

We are not God, but we are good.

The One who made us also blessed us.

The One who made and blessed us became one with us, became one *of* us, because this poverty leaves room for love. This is a poverty that God embraced and fell in love with so fully as to be Incarnate.

"He emptied himself."

"It is not as if we had a high priest who was incapable of feeling our weakness with us. . . . He lives too in the limitations of weakness."

But we are creatures wondrously, fearfully made, endowed with the gift of knowing our creatureliness. We know we are incomplete and frail. We know we can be wounded. This knowledge makes us guarded, this knowledge gives birth to fear.

It is our poverty we fear, our blessed poverty we run from. We hate it so much we would extinguish it if we could.

Wipe it out. Cover it. Elude it. And yet the cost is the loss of our very selves.

Outraged at the fact that we are not God, we are tempted to pretend that we are. We seek to escape the very condition that Christ took upon himself.

"Oh, but he really couldn't have been *truly* human," we might say, "since he didn't sin."

Thus we miss the whole point: the fact of his sinlessness was nothing other than the fact of his being truly, fully, inescapably, and faithfully human.

For all our sin is little other than the negation of our poor but blessed humanness.

This poverty of our creaturehood is often what is meant when people speak of "spiritual" poverty. And yet it is not just a poverty of the spirit in us, but of our whole being, our every experience of love or commitment, of vulnerability or loss, of unguardedness.

It is the poverty which all humans share most profoundly with all those "others" who are usually called "poor."

Jean Vanier has called it "our inability to cope."

Our attempts at "simple lifestyle" or living in a "poor part of the world," or working at a soup-kitchen will never be our deepest and truest identity with the poor. These excursions may be both excellent and desirable for other reasons, but our fullest "solidarity with the poor," no matter how wealthy or destitute we may be, will be our willingness to enter into the mystery of our own unmanageable humanity.

We find it as spouses who, as Goethe said, "become the custodians of one another's solitude," who take the risk of forgiveness, of giving and receiving help.

We find it as parents, facing the unknown of our children's futures, trusting them, entrusting their destiny into God's hands.

We find it as single persons, especially if we feel robbed of spouse or child.

We find it as the terrible unprotectedness of old age and the terrifying openness of youth.

We find it in the awe-ful, awesome moments of shattering love when it feels as though we could die from it — or already have.

We find it in the great unguardedness of true solitude. Or true intimacy.

We enter it with our fears, our great losses — of a child or a promise or a dream.

We encounter it in those who live at the margins of culture and society, for whom all of the pretenses of security and managerial expertise are only a rebuke.

Every instant of faith or of hope or of love, so fragile and fraught with insecurity, is the embodiment of this poverty of our humanness.

It is when we are most weak, indeed.

And it is when we are most strong, most creative, most stunning in beauty, most empty.

"Into your hands, I commend my spirit."

Father Dan

They will miss Father Dan at Alcazar this Christmas. He died at the onset of Advent, so he won't be there to say Mass for his "saints."

That's what he called these reluctant occupants of a "home" for winos, bag ladies, and people not quite mentally ill enough to be institutionalized, and those few sound ones who just had no other place to go. He seemed to look at them all the way that Christ would look at them. And they were made holy by his gaze.

The first time I saw Father Dan say Mass at Alcazar, he taught me a lesson in liturgical music. It was Christmas, so he taught them "Happy Birthday to Jesus" as the opening song. The funny thing about it was; they sang the tune of "Happy Birthday" to everything in the Mass. "Lord Have Mercy on Us" à la "Happy Birthday," "We Offer You Our Gifts" à la "Happy Birthday," "O God We Love You" at the Communion à la "Happy Birthday"; by the end of the celebration they were really roaring. A real birthday party.

His homily was simple: Since Christ became one of us for the love of all of us, they better start treating each other like saints. Even more, since Christ was poor, and not very remarkable in terms of worldly impressiveness, and in so many ways helpless, and born in undesirable surroundings, they especially had reason to be proud at Alcazar.

After Mass he gave out cigarettes and ice cream.

They loved him.

The very few times I was honored to replace him, I could see the disappointment on their faces. It was not the cigarettes or the ice cream: I even brought extras. No, it was Father Dan and his old Air Force chaplain salute. They knew that he loved them.

I saw Father Dan Campbell a few days before he died. He had a hole in his throat and couldn't talk. And he was the only person I've ever seen on one of those machines and yet smiling. It was a terribly short visit, busy as I thought I was; but he gave me a joy made possible only by the deepest of unutterable bonds.

He pointed to his eye. Then his heart. Then to me.

And I was not at all jealous that Father Dan Campbell, to be sure, had told so many others in so many ways that he loved them. He loved me just as surely as he did his saints at Alcazar. It was as real and particular for me as for any mother's child. And for his favorite Mother's Child.

His advent is over. What a Christmas man he was.

Bolen Carter

We had a memorial Mass for Bolen Carter at the Saint Louis Catholic Worker community last night. It was a fitting location.

His life was as devoted to the Eucharist as it was to the poor.

On the wall of the big dining room was a picture of his three modern heroes: Martin Luther King, his hero for civil rights; Dorothy Day, his heroine for a radical Catholic faith; and Gandhi, his hero for nonviolent passive resistance.

It was the Catholic Worker that actually brought Bolen and his wife together. Having read Dorothy Day's paper one day a little over fifty years ago, Bolen rode from East Saint Louis across the river to attend a meeting where he met Anne Loftus. And it was at a Catholic Worker party that they had their first dance. Anne, while not wanting to sound *overly* romantic, remembers that from that moment, "we knew we were in love."

Whenever I visited Bolen and Anne, we would always share the Eucharist. It was another great love of their lives—a love in many ways enkindled by their friend Dorothy Day, who had stayed at their home on visits to Saint Louis long ago.

I will always remember the "prayers of the faithful" the two of them would offer in their little apartment. Bolen, after all our petitions for the world and the church and downcast, would ask for more patience and generosity. Anne would ask for greater simplicity and willingness to love. There was never a time I would leave their home and not feel a surge of hope in God and trust in the human heart.

When I had heard that Bolen died while I was out of the country, I was struck by how impossible it seemed to imagine Bolen and Anne separate from one another. They had truly become as much one body as one mind and heart over the fifty years of Catholic Action, the Cana Conference, retreat work, the labor for racial justice, the five years of Papal Volunteering in Central America.

They were truly one through it all, one in their love for their son John and their daughter Anne, one in the liturgy, one in their sufferings and diminishments, one in their passion for justice, one in prayer, one in joy.

They are supposed to have said one time that Dorothy Day was the saint in their life. That may be true. But truer still was this: the saint in their lives was each other.

They are still inseparable. And Bolen was surely there at the Catholic Worker Mass in his honor.

I was reminded of the words of a young woman married ten years, speaking of her husband: "I don't know where he leaves off and where I begin."

So it was as I looked at Anne there, frail and radiant as a silver candle.

Though Bolen Carter had passed from this earth, half of him was still there with us.

And though Anne is still happily here, half of her is already in heaven.

"I'm So Afraid"

I had been in India six months.

Still, it had not happened.

I had wanted some transformation, some realignment, some sign. Something that might make me different than I am.

How much I had wanted to serve the poor, to be a "man of the poor," to identify with them.

Yet I was still so reluctant, so timid, so unsure.

Even my thirty-day retreat was a fiasco. For the last ten days, about all I could say or think was, "In you, O my God, I trust." Its meagerness disgusted me.

I went to Calcutta. Perhaps that could prove or improve me. Perhaps I might still be like Peter Claver or Francis Xavier or Dorothy Day. But my uncertainty was as large as my fear.

At first meeting Mother Teresa in preparation to work at her "House of the Dying," I asked her to pray for me.

"What do you want?"

"Certitude."

"No, I won't pray for certitude. That is the last thing you have to let go of."

And so I went to work.

On our first early morning trip through the steaming street we picked up four people. One of them was still alive, a knotted-up old Bengali who had been sitting like a pretzel for thirty days, emaciated and caked with Calcutta.

The Sister at the door said to me the words I had secretly dreaded hearing.

"Would you clean him, brother."

And smiling a smile that repressed both agony and guilt I cheerfully answered yes.

As hypochondriacal as I was and as dirty as he was, it turned out to be the easiest task of the day.

By noon I had almost passed out after opening the dressing of a man who had tuberculosis of the bone. Barely making it to the street I propped my feet against a wall and lit a cigarette, hoping to get some blood back to my head.

When I came back in, one of the brothers consoled me with the thought that most people have trouble dealing with the wounds.

After that, they gave me easier tasks: cleaning, grooming, feeding.

And yet it never eased.

Each night I went back to the Jesuit residence thinking I had a new disease—cancer, tuberculosis, syphilis, parasites.

Each night I thanked God that Mother Teresa had not allowed me to stay with the Missionary Brothers in their hard and bare dormitories.

"No, Father, you go to your own community. The last Jesuit who stayed with the Brothers died . . ."

So there I was, after a month, in my little closet-room, rubbed raw by the city, so timid and ashamed—especially by the letters from the States that cooed of my courage and desire to "serve the poor."

I thought if I could make it only another week. . . . But the ache was terrible, and the thought was defeating.

Over and over, I could only say:

"I'm so afraid, and so alone and so cold. . . ."

The next day as I entered the "House of the Dying," the old Bengali, now close to death and full of panic, spotted me as I came through the door.

"Brother! Come to me! Now!

"I'm so afraid and alone, and I'm so cold."

He echoed my own paltry words of the night before, and at that moment, I saw him with new eyes.

He was no longer "the poor" out there, no longer a "problem." He was just like me. He was a brother.

And the weight finally began to lift.

And the fear was finally disarmed.

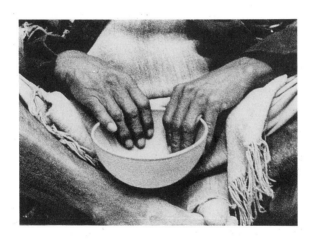

Christopher Robin

There may be some things, perhaps, in the face of which it is best to remain silent.

And yet desire hungers for expression. Feelings, even ineffable ones, want for words.

Christopher Robin lived in a hospital neonatal intensive care unit for two months. Even by the day he died, he had not reached the time for his ordinarily expected birth.

What can one say about the death of anyone, but especially about the death of a beloved innocent? Dostoievsky found it only a source of rage. Bertrand Russell could not touch it with his mind or math; he foundered on its utter irrationality.

But the question of Christopher Robin's tiny little life, his meaning, his mission, persists and wants an answer.

He was, his father wrote, an "early birthday gift" — so precipitously early that every day demanded strategies for survival. But there was a reality to this boy — as fragile as his hold on life might be: "He was brave and determined and stayed with us much longer than expected, so we could get to know him. He was calmed by his parents' voices, smiled after he was fed, and held our hands very tightly."

(At most, it could have only been a finger that Christopher grasped, since his hand print on his memorial card was no bigger than my thumb.)

His mother thanked the people who had helped her son in so short a life, "sending him love and strength, praying for him, washing his body, wiping his face, stroking his forehead, and wishing him well."

The words beckoned me into the deeper meanings of Christopher Robin's existence.

We measure ourselves so often, by what we do and make. Indeed, this is part of our glory, a part we hope that our children live long enough to experience. But a further measure of our being is what we draw out of others, the gifts that they are moved to bestow on us.

And so one young child was wanted in this unwanting world, was passionately desired and hoped for, was affirmed in every hour's struggle, above all, by two people.

In short, he was loved.

And that is all that will ever last of his or any of our lives. This child's reality, his destiny, even his accomplishment was greater than loveless logic can propose.

Christopher Robin, through the love he called out from his mom and dad, made their words of love more fully flesh. No matter what the anguish and heartache—and perhaps, as a measure of it—he made their human desires more real and permanent. He actually caused love and care to blossom which, but for him, would not have flowered in the fall and winter of 1989.

"We will never stop loving him and missing him."

His mother chose the words in his memorial that she had remembered for herself and her baby. And, because of Christopher Robin, the words would be written in a way they had never been meant before or could be written again:

"Yea, though I walk through the valley of the shadow of death, I will fear no evil; for thou art with me. . . ."

Mother and Father, would you have wanted to be spared the anguish and the sorrow, if the price would have been that you had never known and loved him?

Christopher Robin. Bearer of Christ. Promise of spring.

Human Vocation

A vocation is a calling-forth of a person, an unfolding of a human career that starts at the earliest moments of our existence. Vocation bears the concreteness of a developing body, the stuff of genes and womb, of time and place, of family and birth. We are called out into this world, and our calling is unavoidably local: this time, this place. Now.

A vocation is also a struggle. It is the labor of becoming, of working out a mission.

That labor, that mission is love. Paul reminds us in First Corinthians that our adulthood and the fulfillment of all our diverse gifts finds itself in love. This is the highest gift behind all natural talents and specific tasks. If there is not love, there is nothing.

Love, then, is the core. Created by love, started by love, nurtured by love, we are only real and lasting because of love.

Thus, a vocation is not something that merely makes us feel good, nor is it necessarily easy. Neither is life or love. For in both life and in love, vocation becomes real only through struggle, purification, and pain.

And so, a priest, questioning his vocation in crisis, must attend to the forces of his life which have called him forth. He must make himself aware of what has empowered him to bring love into the lives of others. He must attend to what has borne the gift of faith, hope, and charity in his world. The point is not the struggle. The point is, what has given life?

And a spouse, who wonders if he or she should in frustration leave all behind, must at all costs attend to the love in the flesh of the child and be mindful of the life given to others in friendship and bring to memory the promise made in the beloved.

Vocations are questioned at moments of vulnerable crisis. But crisis, that wound of choice, that terrible mark of freedom, is often the very moment of deepening life and love in us.

This is not to say that it is impossible for a profound life-choice to be shifted under the guidance of the Spirit. But I think it is most rare. The long labor of love in crisis is not the dying of a vocation. It may only be the final birth of it.

Those who are basically happy in their vocations have discovered this truth.

Single people who, precisely through the losses they experience, shine as beacons of faith, who offer to others a love that transcends the limits of spouse or child, who reveal the awesome power of abiding friendship, they know this truth.

A single parent, while feeling bereft of intimate fidelity, becomes the sure sign of faithfulness to a child. An adoptive parent, without the consolation of seeing the beloved's eyes in the eyes of the baby, reveals to the sight of all the most consoling parenthood of God.

And married people, who, through great sorrows and joys of long intimacy, remain to say, "I will abide with you in thick and thin, and we will prophesy to the world by the life of the children we bestow on it, by the harbor we will offer to our companions, and by the sharing of our blessings with the poor," they know the truth of being called.

These are vocations. They are utterly unique, utterly irreplaceable, all revealing in concert the voice of God's call. In each one's labor, what lasts of them indelibly through every struggle, is love.

The laborious love that is found in every Christian vocation is the same force at work in vocations to the sisterhood, the priesthood, and brotherhood.

But these are profoundly different vocations than those of the committed single or married life.

My dear "non-believing" friend, Professor Albert William Levi, knew this well. He was confounded and moved by the life of religious sisters, rooted in a faith that does justice, felt in care for the poor, and exercised in a willingness to go anywhere the cry of children is heard. He discovered in them a kind of love which he had not previously seen. It reached beyond family, beyond even the joys of friendship, and far beyond all the so-called "natural explanations" for human motivation—fame, property, family.

Such love is expressed in a life wholly given to solitude before the mystery of God. It is seen in the labors of a parish priest who really has his church and people as his own spouse. It is embodied in religious communities that devote themselves to healing and teaching in total availability.

These vocations are not "higher" than any other. For the only "highest" vocation is love itself, resounding through all our different voices.

But the life of a priest or religious is radically different in its own harrowing moments of poverty.

An eight-year-old girl, quite intelligent and yet quite innocent of faith and religion, looked at me one day with the strangest stare: "Do you have a girlfriend?" "No." "Do you have a wife or kids?" "No." "Do you have a business?" "No."

"Then you must be nobody."

As painful as it was to hear it, I realized that she saw something that many in religious life or priesthood seem to have forgotten. Our life *should* make no sense without Christ. Such a life, in its core, is so radical, it is meaningless without faith.

Indeed, a sister, a brother, a priest, ought to be "a nobody" if there is not a love that flowers in service, simplicity, and a willingness to respond anywhere to the wounds of humanity. And indeed we should feel our lives as nothing if that Love is not encountered in the silent citadel of an ordinary man or woman alone before God.

We live out, by the relinquishments of our lives, a wider range of God's love than could be imagined without us. So it is with all vocations.

The happiest people, whether single, married, parents, priest, sister, or brother, are happy not only because they have found themselves. They are happy because they have made a singular and irreplaceable divestment.

Having found themselves, they gave themselves away.

They have been called.

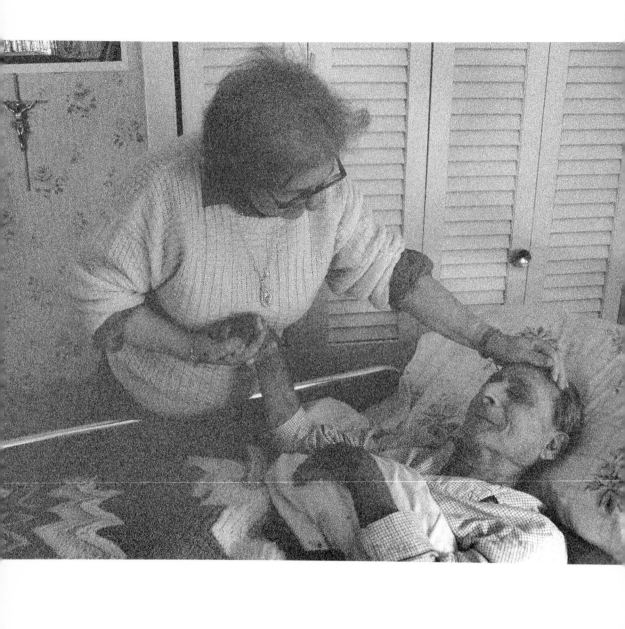

The Toe Woman

In the year following my father's death, his widow got much advice. "Get away from it all."

"Take a vacation."

"Go out and have some fun."

And yet, it was enough for her to sit on her front porch. It was the one my father had remodeled. It was a good reminder. And she liked his presence as much as the feel of the place, the yard, the street.

But there was a weight to her. A quietness. An inactivity that might have led one to believe that she was at least mildly depressed.

Then she read in the parish bulletin, nine or ten months later, that a family was looking for someone to stay with their mother three nights a week. It seemed the woman rarely slept, struck by "Lou Gehrig's Disease," unable to move anything of her frail body but her toe.

My mother inquired. And then backed off.

"I asked about the situation, but I think I ought to turn this one down. I'll have to feed her through a hole in her stomach and give her care that I don't think I'd like. I could do those things for my own kids when they were babies, but not in this case."

And yet, with chiding encouragement, she gave it a shot. She would try to do the job for at least a week and then stop if it turned out to be too difficult.

Well, the "toe" woman and her family were something to think about. They had taught her to communicate with them by the movement of her toe. They would ask, "Is the first letter from "a" to "e"—and if it were, they would say "a . . . b . . . c . . ." and if she moved her toe, the first letter of the first word would be "c."

My mother was touched by their love for her—but more by her love for them and especially for her husband.

She recalled that even though she did not mind giving the woman food through a syringe into her stomach, it was clear to her how much more it was appreciated when the husband, with his own touch, seemed to delight the paralyzed woman.

After a few months, my mother remarked on how much she wished she could be like the toe-woman. "She has such a smile and she seems to appreciate even the littlest thing."

That she would hope to be *like* her: a woman paralyzed and unable even to taste the food that nourished her, a woman who represented the powerlessness and dependency that we all endlessly fear, was not enough.

One June night — among all those nights of conversations, rosaries and laughter — the toe-woman spelt out: "I . . . . L . . . O . . . V . . . E . . . . Y . . . O . . . U . . .

Months later, near the vigil of her death, the woman who was paralyzed spelt out to the woman who helped her: "I . . . T . . . . H . . . A . . . S . . . . B . . . E . . . E . . . N . . . . A . . . . G . . . R . . . E . . . A . . . T . . . . P . . . R . . . I . . . V . . . I . . . L . E . . G . . . E . . . . T . . . O . . . . K . . . N . . . O . . . W . . . .

But the woman who helped said no. It was quite the opposite.

And she meant it.

For who was paralyzed and then empowered to walk with joy and grace?

Who was imprisoned and then made free?

Who was blind and finally saw?

Saw, yes, that if the only thing you can do in the world is move your toe, you can change the human heart.

And change the world.

Handicapped

There was something that held us back from visiting Van for those six months. A great athlete, a fine scholar and leader, a teacher of us all, we kept saying that we wanted to see him; but we seemed never to be able to bring ourselves to do it.

I think we were afraid.

Van had had a stroke. The last time I had seen him was in a hospital, just prior to his being transported out to a nursing home in the country. It was so hard to look at him—just a slump and a vacant stare.

And so, although we felt we should visit Van, we really didn't want to. I think it was that in some way we did not want to see our own destiny.

But guilt, I guess, won the better of us. The four of us finally journeyed forth: a lawyer, a psychologist, a theologian, a teacher of philosophy. Very active people. Busy about many things.

When we caught sight of him, peering in from the antiseptic hall, we knew that there was not much point. He seemed not to know we had come until we started talking loudly, shaking his hands, chattering about the Saint Louis Cardinals and how "well" Van looked.

The conversation, high and fast, was really across Van rather than to him. He made no response. Nothing to say. The most he could do was drag on a cigarette, if you lit one and put it in his mouth. Or sip from a cup of water.

What to do?

"How about Mass?" we said. "Would you like to have Mass?"

And of course, not even expecting a response from him, we draped him in a stole and at least had something to keep us busy for half an hour.

At the Consecration, it seemed as if Van would speak. But all that he did was open his mouth to drool. We wiped it and moved on, finishing quietly, gathering ourselves, preparing, anticipating.

It is so difficult when you cannot manage. When you don't know what to do next, when you are in the unfathomable reaches of human mystery.

"Well, it was great to see you, Van. We'll come again."

And as we shook his hand to make our leaving sure and easy, he held on to each of our hands. He brought them to his mouth. He kissed them. And he wept.

With what little part of his brain he could engage and command, he bestowed that gift on us.

And I have never doubted since then that all of us are handicapped. All of us are brain-damaged, wounded, helpless kids, hidden old men and women.

It's just that some of us can pretend better than others.

"A New Path"

I feel like I'm walking down a new path. It's not physical fear or fear of death, because the courageous poor in Latin America have taught me a theology of life that, through solidarity and our common struggle, transcends death. Rather, it is a sense of helplessness—that I, who always wanted to be the champion of the poor, am just as helpless—that I, too, must hold out my begging bowl; that I must learn—am learning—the ultimate powerlessness of Christ. It is a cleansing experience. So many things seem less important, or not at all, especially the ambitions. Peace and love, Penny.

—Penny Lernoux
letter to friends as she was dying of cancer

V

DIVINE HUMANIZATION

Come to me
All you who labor
And are overburdened

And I will give you rest.

Take up my yoke
And learn from me
For I am gentle
And humble of heart

And you will find rest for your souls.

Yes, my yoke is easy
And my burden is light.

— *Matthew 11:28–30*

The Face of Christ Poor

The face of poverty, like all the faces of humanity, must be encountered in all of its appearances.

Every part of a face has meaning only in relation to the other parts and the whole face itself.

The face is a "field" rather than a conglomeration or mere addition of isolated segments. Every part is defined by its mutuality with the other parts. You cannot understand any face if you fixate on only one part to the exclusion of the others.

A face is a dynamic field, like a baseball field. You never understand baseball by only examining what a pitcher is and does. The whole meaning of the pitcher is dependent upon the pitcher's relationship to the batter, catcher, defense, time frame, score. And yet, without the pitcher, you have no game of baseball.

A human face is not a strung-out series of two eyes, a nose, two ears, and a mouth. Their position in relationship to each other is crucial. The whole face is precisely the relationship. And the mutuality of the parts is what is so compelling about the face one gazes on.

So it is with the faces of poverty, the faces of the poor, and the face of Christ.

The finding and following of "Christ poor" is a multi-dimensional experience, just as Jesus' own poverty had many dimensions.

He came to heal the wound of the dehumanized poor, even to heal the wound of death. This is why he is found in the face of the destitute. We must see his face there or we will never see the whole Christ, nor will our discipleship ever be whole-hearted. In this realm, he calls us to labor with him in the mission of healing through justice, compassion, our professional lives, and our direct service.

Jesus travelled light. The person for others. His simplicity was single-mindedness. He had nowhere to "lay his head"—not because he had a distaste for material things, but because he was so fully emptied and open to the One who sent him, the One who abides in each human tabernacle. Thus he had no encumbrances. Thus, he would celebrate at Cana, bless wine, marvel at Zaccheus, rest at Bethany. His "material" poverty—a poverty that humanizes us—was a function only of his love.

And it was the undying love of God for us, revealed in Jesus, which brought him face to face with the poverty of sin—the false riches of mind and body, the false idols, the false escapes, the negation and pretense. He is found in the very recognition of our own sinfulness—a spiritual poverty which dehumanizes and destroys us only if we refuse to look at it.

"Depart from me, I'm a sinner."

"Come follow me."

Finally, the face of Jesus is found in the truth of our humanity. His face is our own, our frail personhood, our wondrous heart and our passion for truth. His spirit stirs in our every vulnerable act of faith, our every tenuous hope, our every bold love. His face is even in the voiceless, whose only yes is the movement of a toe.

The totality is the issue: Poverty in all of its presentations, in all of its faces, is the appearance of the face of Jesus.

If there is a preferential option for the poor, it must be present to the whole face.

This indeed may be the crisis of a country which ignores the sea of human suffering, which mounts a myth of personal and national invulnerability, which is glutted on a feast of things, which denies its own sin.

This may be the crisis of a church which, so strong, searches out again its very intelligibility and mission, which is tempted to offer rules or dogma or achievement or self-righteousness as salvation instead of the radical trust in Christ's redemptive gift.

This could be our own crisis of faith as well, squeezing the dynamic totality of poverty into only one of its appearances and ignoring all the rest.

An evangelical faith in Christ, which is in its deepest reality an inescapable and irreplaceable option for the poor, will be unleashed in us only when we gaze, finally unguarded, upon

the face of the devastated, whom we would touch
the face of simplicity in personal presence
the face of the one who sees and loves us even in our sin
and the face of our precious but frightening vulnerability.

Fall

I think my mind will always, at the autumn time of year, drift to an old Jesuit.

The letting go of fall,
 the relinquishment of harvesting
 the giving of gratitudes
 the anticipation of winter
all call back the image of that old man
 running around the lawn
 collecting leaves in his hands
 weeping and kissing the trees.

That is how I remember the story. He is now dead, so I cannot confirm it.

Yet even if he were alive to tell the tale, he wouldn't be able to inform me whether the story were true or false.

You see, he had lost his memory almost totally, so he wouldn't have been able to remember what had happened the previous fall.

He wouldn't have been able to remember that there had been a spring.

The man lived totally in the present. In the presence.

Not by gift of mysticism, but by erosion of the body. And so when the leaves started falling each fall, it was the end of the world for him.

The trees were dying.

The earth was ending.

No wonder it was an occasion for such tender handling of the leaves and embracing of the earth.

Having lost his memory, he had won that sweet and painfully overwhelming sense of the present.

To savor, to relish, to give thanks.

How easy to lose the simple present.

We replay the past, rehearse the future as some kind of conscious armor against the terribly fleeting present.

We hope not to feel the hurt of impermanence as much, but we've unfortunately traded off our childlike and ancient sensitivity for the eternal now.

We suffer the delusion that if we hold ourselves back from caring too much, we will never feel the damage of the loved one now lost.

We pass. We are passing away. And this dear earth passes.

But there is now.

To kiss the falling leaves.

To embrace the trees.

The point is not to fear the regret of having meant so much to someone that absence might bring pain.

The point is not to protect ourselves from loving this present earth, this present face, but to let our hearts be indeed broken

by each earthly departure,

by all dear separations,

by every aching distance.

For it is a breaking open, a wound, a poorness of love that fills us with Love's very self.

As C.S. Lewis sang:

> For this I bless you as the rain falls.
> The pains you give me
> are more precious
> than all other gains.

A Radical Devotion

She thought that a believer feels a bond with others who have struggled
with life's mysteries. The saints, for her, were men and women who
had waged such a struggle, and their losses, their pain and uncertainty,
as well as their victories, their moments of moral satisfaction or religious ecstasy, are an inheritance from which all of us are eligible to
draw.

The psychiatrist Robert Coles offers a profound testament of friendship
and holiness in *Dorothy Day: A Radical Devotion*.

His bond with Dorothy Day was sealed when, as a young doctor whose
wife was deathly ill for weeks in a hospital, he received daily letters of prayer
and encouragement from the great social activist and co-founder of the
Catholic Worker.

Based upon this friendship which had extended back into Coles's young
life as a visitor at the Catholic Worker and continued over the years until
Dorothy's death in her eighties, his revelation of her life and labor is itself
as much an embodiment of the purifications and joys of relationship as the
life of the woman he presents.

Dorothy Day is so truly a saint for our time—offering to us the same
inheritance of grace that she seems always to have received from her favorite
saints. Her devotion to the poor is both mystical and profoundly realistic.
Her sense of justice is totally grounded in the inescapable commands of
Christ and reaches out to the social, political, and economic world with
relentless consistency. Her love of the church—through all of its glory and
despite all of its sin—is breathtaking in the face of all those who would
refashion it in some other image than that of Christ.

But what I found most splendid about this woman —which only Robert

Coles's book has been able to reveal—is how she, at his request, evaluated and summarized what mattered in her life.

This woman, who lived through so many turmoils, loves, and labors of her youth; who knew the great and famous; who, with Peter Maurin, founded one of the most significant communitarian movements in the history of American Catholicism; who picketed, protested, and petitioned for the poor; who lived through the passing of presidents and popes; who maintained her faith during years of almost numbing transition and change; who had inspired many thousands to lives of service and hundreds to risk imprisonment as she did for the sake of truth; who could energize a crowd by the quiet, riveting, purposefulness of her voice, summed up what was most significant about her life in these words:

> I was going to try to make a summary for myself, write what mattered most—but I couldn't do it. I just sat there and thought of our Lord, and his visit to us all those centuries ago, and I said to myself that my great luck was to have had him on my mind for so long in my life.

When I first met Dorothy Day, over twenty-five years ago, I think I saw in her eyes what her dear friend Robert Coles heard in her words: not only the fire of a radical devotion, but the freedom of a person who realized that the most privileged and prized gift she might make to the world and to her God was the poverty of her longing, human heart.

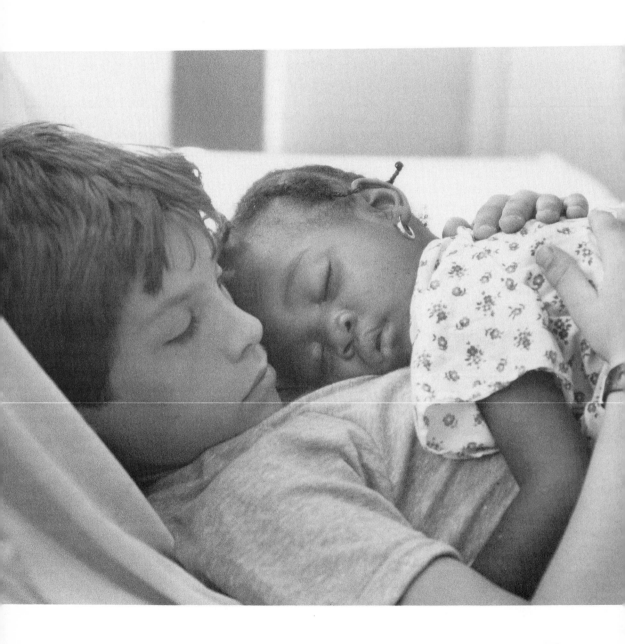

Word Made Flesh

What was he like? He was human, we know that. He once had been a baby. We also believe he was and is God.

If you can believe that a baby in a crib is God, you can believe anything. Even that God could look like bread and taste like wine.

We don't realize how crazy our faith is. "Mary had a baby. My Lord!" If you can believe that, you can believe that the person next to you is as sacred as the Blessed Sacrament.

And poor Joseph. Everything went wrong. Everything you would want for your own child fell through. First of all, the baby wasn't even really his. Then, he couldn't even provide him the best of homes. A barn, of all things. And on top of all that, they were out to get him.

Could God really have been a baby? Could God have really been nursed by Mary? The great painters tell it so. Was he a boy? Truly? With all that goes into boyness—and not just snails and puppy dog tails?

Could he really have been like my nephews? Or was God just playing "Let's Pretend"? Was he trying to make his way through this strange world, trying to find it out and manage and tame it? Or did he know the whole score and never have to feel the pains of uncertainty?

Was he really a teenager? Did he have desires? Fears? Plans to get even? Is it possible that he could have loved a woman? Some novelists say so. But the gospels never say.

Perhaps it's best we not know too much about him. In fact, the more I think about it, the more confounding it is to believe that he is the very word of God made flesh. How could human flesh be godly anyway? How could a baby be eternal, wisdom, consoler, and counselor?

We all seem to have this unquestioned pretense that it was so clear, so evident and undeniable.

Well, I think it would have been an awful challenge to believe in him. That baby? Could I have really believed with Mary? Could I have accepted it all with Joseph? Could I have travelled so far, my feet on the ground and my eyes on the heavens with the Magi? Could I have really believed that God was speaking in dreams and stars and holy innocence?

Most shepherds would have stayed asleep. Or at least minded the sheep. What would the boss say? And if I had been the prophetess Anna, I would have given up hoping long ago. If Simeon, I would have felt so sorry for myself, I probably wouldn't have even noticed the Holy Family coming in.

They were so commonplace, so distressingly and embarrassingly ordinary to be Holy.

If only he could have sprung full-grown from the head of Zeus, like our more impressive gods. If only he had been born into royalty. If only, as an infant, he could perform star wars on Herod and his minions.

But no, he had to insist upon being one of us.

If you can believe that you can believe anything. Even that we might in the end prevail, by God's kind favor. Even that birth, not death, might be the last word.

If you can believe in Christmas, you're lucky.

If you can believe in that, you can move mountains. But you must see that such belief can only be born of our human frailty — and the embrace of it.

Good Friday

As often as that most Good of Fridays will return for me, I will remember one of my first directed retreats. I was apprehensive, even fearful, as the eight days of solitude got under way. I guess I had always expected that God might have something terrible to say to me, something embarrassing and humiliating, or even something too challenging for me to bear. Until that time, my spirituality had often been reduced to two apprehensive questions: "What bad news has God found out about me now?" and "What is God going to ask next?"

And so, in this particular retreat, I was again hesitant. I knew that Jesus had once said, "Fear is useless; what you need is trust." But I guess I thought that such kindness applied only to Christ's contemporaries.

I told my retreat director of my fears. And he asked a most mysterious question: "John, what are the two most universal pictures we Catholics have of our God?"

I always feel on the spot when asked questions like that, so I fumbled around in my memory and came up with "a triangle" and "a circle." Christ must have thought I was a hopeless case.

"No, no," my director said. "Come on; what are the two dominant images of God that we have which are everywhere and which have been immortalized by our artists for two thousand years?"

Well, since he gave me the hint, I got a little smarter. "The Sacred Heart?" "The Good Shepherd?"

He gave me a blank stare. "John: don't you know? A defenseless baby in a manger and a defenseless man on a cross. Now tell me: What are you afraid of when you go before such a God?"

The retreat was splendid. Sure, I knew my sinfulness; but I knew, more than I had ever known before, how much God loves us.

That, after all, is what Good Friday is all about.

It is not about fear and guilt. It is not about devastation and embarrassment. It is not about hate and revenge. It is about love. It is about God.

I remember being told, as a grade-schooler, that our sins contributed directly to the anguish of Jesus on the Cross.

So-called wiser minds came along and told me otherwise. Surely, such an attitude did little credit to God and just made us feel like sludge.

Well, in a way, both judgments are correct. We are not sludge. And God is not a tyrant.

No, we are priceless. And God is a "tremendous lover."

And yet, there is a way in which our own sinful infidelities add to the anguished suffering of Christ who is in and beyond all time. We do this, I believe, by denying the two great arms of the crucifixion.

When you think of the meaning of God's love for us in Jesus Christ, there come to mind two radical rejections of that love which must indeed cause suffering to the crucified Christ.

You see, God so loved us, even in our sinful poverty, as to become one with our own sinful condition, to die with us, like us and for us. That's how valuable we humans are. That's how needy we are.

And the two screaming rejections of such love are these:

"No, I am not worth your death. I was not worth your life and love. I am not worth your efforts, your forgiveness, your suffering, your passion." This is the response we give when we are so overcome by our own sin that we think it is greater than God's creation, more lasting than God's love, and more compelling than God's beauty.

The second response is even more tragic:

"Thanks, but no thanks. You see, I did not need your love. I do not need your suffering and your bleeding heart. I do not want your forgiveness and your redeeming labors. For I am a 'self-made' person. I did it on my own. I pulled myself up by my own bootstraps. The others may need your death, your love, but not me."

And so the two arms of the cross are cut off by the hardened human attitudes that we were either not worth Christ's life, death, and resurrection, or that we really had no need of him.

The Friday of Christ's death was not "Guilty Friday" or "Gruesome Friday." It was a Friday of Goodness: the Goodness of God and the goodness of us all. We can only add to the suffering of God by denying our sinfulness as well as our goodness.

There is no one of us so virtuous who does not need—desperately—God's loving forgiveness.

And there is no one among us so sinful who is not worth—endlessly—such a lavish gift.

If we know these truths, we will never die.

And we need never fear.

Eamon Casey

He was a bishop.

He had much experience, many gifts.

And yet, as I spoke to him, he insisted that he had learned more about life, about being a bishop, and about faith in ten minutes than he had learned in ten years.

Like so many men and women, he sympathized with the poor, he spoke for justice, he had given service.

He also knew those on the front line; so well, that he had received a letter from Archbishop Romero the very week in which the Salvadoran prelate was assassinated.

He said it seemed so clear to him that one of the Irish bishops had to go to the funeral, to stand somehow in solidarity with Romero and his people. The killers had obliterated Romero at Mass, as if to say: "Stay away, keep your Christ and his blood out of our lives, our world, our business."

He proposed the funeral pilgrimage to his fellow bishops, well aware that this might be seen simply as one more of Casey's excuses to travel. There were even jokes about it:

What's the difference between God and Eamon Casey?
God is everywhere, but Casey is only everywhere except Galway.

Having stuck out his neck, the rope tightened. In the absence of other volunteers, Casey, the bishop of Galway, would be sent to Romero's funeral.

My remembered fragments of his account:

The day of the burial was astounding.
Thousands were in the square, most of them poor.

Soldiers were ominously planted on the roof-tops.
And then the bombs went off.
There was a huge vacancy in the square.
All that you could see were shoes.
The people surged like a tidal wave, pushing
the bishops back against the cathedral and
pinning them to the wall.
I thought I would die, suffocate —
pressed by the poor against the walls of the church.
I made an act of contrition
and an act of love and faith in Jesus Christ.
And then I became a free man.

In solidarity with the people of Salvador, in grieving for their Archbishop, in letting go of all life and plans and security, at the moment of feeling crushed even to death, in that splendid confluence of political passion, personal commitment, and holy abandonment. Liberation struck.

Another person of faith and hope and love, beyond all words and seminars, beyond all tutors and books, beyond all programs and sermons, beyond all the kindnesses and services, had seen anew and differently and definitively the Face of Christ.

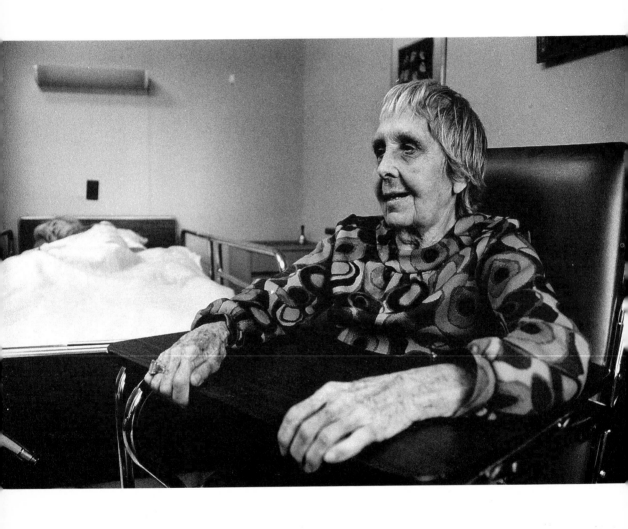

Edwina

The last time I saw her, the disease, which claims and incapacitates her body progressively, had moved from her shoulders so that she could no longer use her hands and arms.

She could still talk, but she was diminished down to buzzing for help by pulling the call-cord with her teeth.

Now she was already planning for future conversations when her power of voice might leave her.

"When I wink with my right eye, that means yes."

Edwina Carey, a Sister of Mercy, still lives.
After the manner of the body.
But somehow she has already died and risen.

When I first saw her while I was giving a retreat in New Orleans, she said from her braced-up chair, all stiff and stern: "You speak like you know a lot about suffering, young man; that's awfully confident."

As is so often the case, I had spoken; someone else had lived.

She knew my lack.

She knew the truth I could only mutter.

It was not until she lost so many of her powers, not until she could no longer teach, not until she relinquished so many gifts of leadership and activism

that she was fully appreciative of her gift

that she realized profoundly what was hers to bestow.

"When I wink my right eye, it means yes."

I left her, that first time, somehow unafraid of anything.
I soon returned with two roses.
One for the cross.
One for the resurrection.

An incident, among many, of death and rising:
She once heard of a woman who was ashamed to have anyone visit her husband, a multiple sclerosis sufferer himself.
Edwina requested to be taken to the couple's apartment.
"I have the same disease as your husband," Sister Edwina said to the reluctant wife blocking the door. "May I come in to talk?"
The woman agreed to let her in, but not to see the husband.
Edwina's wheelchair would not fit the threshold, so she asked the woman to prop her up against the wall while the folded chair could be slipped through the door.
And so the whole world would see Edwina Carey slowly sliding down the wall, the woman straining mightily to hold her up, the wheelchair barely making it through the door for the nun to fall into it.
The world laughed.
Including the wife.
"You can see my husband."

Edwina does this for you.
I look forward to seeing her again, such is my need.
I walk into her presence and some strange cellar of fear and apprehension is unlocked in me.
Some great light, a boldness of faith seeps in.
This woman has handed everything over—so that even the slightest move is something transcendent.
No longer having a tightened grip on reality, her life is an open hand.
It holds you.
And when she can no longer move her lips to the words of life's consecration, she is prepared.
It will be in her face.
She will wink with her right eye to say yes.

The Face

We look.
Our eyes search.
   Will it be at some other time?
   Might it be in some other place?
Where is poverty?
Where are the poor?
How might we find and follow the Poor One?
Who are the blessed?

"The poor you will always have with you."

The face of the Poor One is
   in the stare of the starving,
   in the darkened eye of the criminal,
   in the last nod of the dying.

The face is found when there is time and uncluttered space
   for the present moment,
   for the present person,
   for the present,
   when securities have not become prisons,
   when goods have not drugged us into forgetfulness,
   when distraction has not robbed us.

The face is found in the search of the penitent,
   in the hope of the sinner,
   in the expectancy of repentance,

in the promise of conversion,
in the one who sees my face, who knows my truth
and loves it.

The face is in the rapt gaze of the beloved,
in the the smile of the mother, who against all
logic, security, and safety, has brought her
harrowingly defenseless child into birth,
in the glance of Dante, stunned by Beatrice,
in the yes of a friend of sixty years,
in the trust of a teenager's father,
in the tears of the griever.

The face of Christ is found fully when the eyes finally see,
when the head is finally turned
back to the truth of poverty,
of who we really are
and are meant to be.

The poor, my friends, are those who need another, those who lack
anything whatever, who come naked before God and in need. The poor,
my friends, are who we all must become.

—Vincent de Paul

"Faces"

For Christ
plays
in ten thousand places,
Lovely in limbs,
and lovely in eyes not his
   —Gerard Manley Hopkins
    "As Kingfishers Catch Fire"

Photographer's Note

Several years ago, I wrote a "creed" of why I take pictures:

> This camera lens is the eye of my soul
> through which I touch the world
> through which the world touches me.
> It captures and carries
> terror and tenderness
> anguish and innocence to eyes that
> otherwise may never see.
>
> At times I ask:
> Dare I invade their lives, steal this moment?
> Yet, how can I not
> share these children with the world?
> How can I not
> bring them to hearts who might receive them
> to voices who might speak for them?

As is evident in this poem, I have long wrestled with the invasive nature of photographing people, especially the poor. I constantly risk offending, humiliating, and violating the very people I seek to serve. Notice the violence suggested by photographic language: we "shoot pictures," after we "load" film and "aim" the camera. I enter this risk of the photographic endeavor, vigilantly nurturing a reverence for persons—a reverence I hope my photos embody.

In contrast to my earlier "creed," I no longer see photography merely as a catalyst to make us, the viewers, voices for the voiceless. Rather, these images are vehicles to help amplify the muted voices of the marginalized. Images can make present what is absent and invite us to speak *with*, not just for, others.

I am grateful for John Kavanaugh's stories which invite us to wake up, to repent, and to celebrate. More than just helping us understand "poverty," his words invite us into a relationship with poor persons, with the poor Christ. John's preaching and teaching of the gospel have shaped my vision since my teen years, when I first began photographing. His reflections remind me of the purpose of these images: to open our eyes and hearts to recognize the face of God in all persons and places.

A Boston photographer who works alongside the poor of Guatemala recently said, "In English we speak of 'taking' a photo. Hopefully, taking photos is for me a way to give back to the people who have given so much to me. Hopefully, this photo exhibit is not about me, but about the people photographed."

I echo what he says and add: the photos in this book are not just about me, nor are they just about the people photographed. These images are about each one of you who gazes on them, you who are among the ten thousand beloved faces in whom Christ is revealed.

— MEV PULEO

Index of Photographs